Ecclesiasticus

(The Wisdom of Jesus the Son of Sirach)

Timeless Teachings on Virtue, Wisdom, and Faith

A Modern Translation

Adapted for the Contemporary Reader

Jesus ben Sirach

Translated by Tim Zengerink

Table Of Contents

Preface - Message to the Reader

What If You Could Help Rebuild the Greatest Library in Human History?

Thousands of years ago, the Library of Alexandria stood as the crown jewel of human achievement — a sanctuary where the collected wisdom of every known civilization was gathered, preserved, and shared freely.

And then, it was lost.

Through fire, conquest, and the slow erosion of time, humanity lost not just books — but ideas, dreams, discoveries, and stories that could have changed the world forever.

Today, the Library of Alexandria lives again — and you are invited to be a part of its restoration.

Our mission is simple yet profound:

To rebuild the greatest library the world has ever known, and to translate all timeless works into every language and dialect, so that no seeker of knowledge is ever left behind again.

By joining our movement to rebuild the modern Library of Alexandria, you become part of an unprecedented mission:

- **Unlimited Access to the Greatest Audiobooks & eBooks Ever Written:**

  Instantly explore thousands of legendary works—Plato, Shakespeare, Jane Austen, Leo Tolstoy, and countless more. All instantly available to read or listen, placing a complete literary universe at your fingertips.

- **Beautiful Paperback & Deluxe Editions at Printing Cost**

  Own any title as an elegant paperback, deluxe hardcover, or stunning collectible boxset—offered to you at true printing cost, delivered straight to your door. Build your personal Library of Alexandria, crafted for beauty, built for durability, and worthy of proud display.

- **Fresh Translations for Modern Readers—in Every Language & Dialect**

  Enjoy timeless masterpieces reimagined in clear, contemporary language—no more outdated phrases or obscure references. Alongside the original versions, we're tirelessly translating these classics into every language and dialect imaginable, ensuring accessibility and understanding across cultures and generations.

- **Join a Global Renaissance of Literature & Knowledge**

  You directly support expanding our library, publishing deluxe editions at true cost, translating works into all global languages, and bringing humanity's greatest stories to people everywhere. By joining today, you're not just preserving a legacy of masterpieces; you set in motion a powerful wave of literary accessibility.

Become a Torchbearer of Knowledge.

Join us for free now at **LibraryofAlexandria.com**

Together, we will ensure that the light of human wisdom never fades again.

With gratitude and a shared love of knowledge,

The Modern Library of Alexandria Team

Visit:

www.libraryofalexandria.com

Or scan the code below:

Introduction

Timeless Teachings on Virtue, Wisdom, and Faith

From ancient civilizations to modern society, humanity has continually sought wisdom—insights that illuminate our path, deepen our understanding, and guide our choices. Among the rich heritage of wisdom literature, Ecclesiasticus, also known as The Wisdom of Jesus the Son of Sirach, stands out as one of the most profound and practical works of ethical, spiritual, and philosophical reflection ever composed.

Written by the Jewish sage Jesus ben Sirach in the second century BCE, Ecclesiasticus is a remarkable compilation of practical advice, moral teachings, spiritual reflections, and profound insights into human nature and divine truth. It offers readers timeless lessons applicable to every area of life, from ethical behavior and personal relationships to spiritual growth and community leadership.

Historical and Cultural Background

Ecclesiasticus originated during a vibrant and tumultuous period in Jewish history. Composed in Hebrew by Jesus ben Sirach, an esteemed teacher and scholar, the text was later translated into Greek by his grandson, making it widely accessible throughout the Hellenistic world. Its Greek title, Ecclesiasticus—meaning "Church Book"—reflects its extensive use within early Christian communities, highlighting its enduring significance across diverse religious traditions.

Jesus ben Sirach lived and taught in Jerusalem, a city at the crossroads of cultural, philosophical, and religious influences. During his lifetime, the Jewish community grappled with the challenges posed by Greek cultural dominance and shifting political landscapes. Amidst these challenges, Sirach's writings offered clarity, stability, and profound guidance rooted in Jewish tradition and universal wisdom.

Literary Style and Structure

Ecclesiasticus is celebrated for its poetic elegance, structured wisdom sayings, and rich metaphorical imagery. Organized primarily as a collection of ethical proverbs, philosophical discourses, prayers, and hymns, the text blends practical advice with profound spiritual reflection. Its accessible yet profound style allows readers to easily engage with its teachings, finding immediate relevance and applicability to daily life.

The structure of Ecclesiasticus emphasizes key virtues, moral principles, and spiritual truths through distinct sections, each addressing specific themes such as wisdom, humility, family life, friendship, leadership, justice, and piety. This clear and structured presentation facilitates deep contemplation, personal reflection, and practical application, making the text an invaluable resource for moral and spiritual growth.

Core Themes and Timeless Insights

Ecclesiasticus covers a diverse range of topics, each providing essential insights into leading a fulfilling, virtuous, and spiritually enriched life. Key themes include:

1. The Pursuit of Wisdom

Central to Sirach's teachings is the profound importance of wisdom, not merely as intellectual knowledge but as spiritual insight and moral discernment. Wisdom, according to Sirach, originates in reverence for God and guides individuals toward ethical behavior, righteous living, and meaningful relationships. The pursuit of wisdom is depicted as a lifelong journey, essential for personal growth and community harmony.

2. Ethical Conduct and Personal Integrity

Ecclesiasticus provides extensive guidance on ethical behavior and personal integrity. It emphasizes virtues such as honesty, humility, generosity, compassion, and respect, highlighting their importance for individual character development and social cohesion. Readers are encouraged to internalize these virtues deeply, allowing ethical principles to inform all aspects of daily life.

3. Faith and Trust in the Divine

Sirach underscores the significance of faith, trust, and reverence toward God as the foundation of true wisdom and virtuous living. He emphasizes that genuine spiritual devotion involves heartfelt trust and active commitment to divine teachings, encouraging readers to cultivate deeper faith and reliance on God's wisdom and providence.

4. Family and Social Relationships

Significant portions of Ecclesiasticus are dedicated to family dynamics, friendships, and community relationships. Sirach offers practical advice on nurturing strong, respectful, and loving relationships, emphasizing mutual support, understanding, forgiveness, and loyalty. These teachings underscore the importance of harmonious relationships as essential for personal happiness and community stability.

5. Leadership and Justice

Ecclesiasticus provides profound insights into ethical leadership and justice. Sirach highlights the responsibilities of leaders to act with integrity, fairness, and humility, advocating principles of justice, compassion, and moral accountability. These teachings remain highly relevant, offering valuable guidance for contemporary leaders across all fields.

Contemporary Relevance

Despite its ancient origins, Ecclesiasticus remains strikingly relevant to contemporary readers, providing invaluable wisdom for navigating modern life's complexities. Its teachings address timeless human concerns, offering guidance on ethical dilemmas, interpersonal relationships, spiritual growth, and moral leadership.

Practical Guidance for Daily Life: Sirach's straightforward advice on ethical conduct, family relationships, and personal integrity provides practical, actionable insights for contemporary life, encouraging thoughtful reflection and virtuous living.

Spiritual Enrichment: The text's profound reflections on faith, divine wisdom, and spiritual devotion resonate deeply with individuals seeking spiritual depth, meaningful connection with the divine, and a purposeful life rooted in faith.

Ethical Leadership and Community Building: Ecclesiasticus emphasizes qualities essential for ethical leadership and community harmony, including justice, humility, compassion, and moral accountability. These principles continue to inspire and inform leaders today.

The Importance of This Modern Translation

This modern translation of Ecclesiasticus ensures its timeless wisdom remains accessible, engaging, and relevant for contemporary readers. Complex ideas, archaic expressions, and cultural references have been carefully adapted to clear, relatable language without sacrificing the depth, beauty, and spiritual richness of the original text.

By bridging the gap between ancient insights and contemporary experience, this adaptation invites readers from diverse backgrounds—scholars, spiritual seekers, or individuals navigating life's challenges—to engage deeply and meaningfully with Sirach's teachings.

The translation provides an approachable and profound entry point into timeless wisdom, enriching readers' moral understanding, spiritual insight, and practical living.

Engaging with Ecclesiasticus: Personal Reflections

As you journey through Ecclesiasticus, approach the text not merely as historical literature but as a living source of personal and spiritual reflection. Each chapter and verse invites you to examine your beliefs, values, actions, and relationships critically, inspiring deep contemplation and personal transformation.

Reflect upon Sirach's teachings, considering how they resonate with your personal experiences, ethical challenges, spiritual questions, and aspirations. Allow this wisdom to challenge, inspire, and guide you toward greater clarity, purpose, and spiritual fulfillment.

Embrace the Journey into Wisdom

Ecclesiasticus stands as an enduring testament to the timeless power and profound relevance of ancient wisdom. Its teachings on virtue, faith, wisdom, and human relationships transcend historical boundaries, offering profound insights for contemporary life.

Translated by Tim Zengerink

May your exploration of this transformative text enrich your faith, deepen your ethical understanding, and inspire you to lead a life characterized by wisdom, virtue, and purpose. Begin your journey into Ecclesiasticus, discovering insights and lessons that can profoundly transform your perspective, character, and spiritual journey.

Chapter 1

All wisdom comes from the Lord and stays with Him forever. Who can count the grains of sand on the shore, the drops of rain, or the endless days of time? Who can measure the sky above, the earth below, the depths of the sea, or the vastness of wisdom?

Wisdom was created before everything else, and understanding has always existed. Who has found where wisdom begins? Who has fully understood her deep knowledge? There is only one who is truly wise and worthy of great respect—the Lord. He created wisdom, observed her, and measured her. He spread wisdom across all He created and freely gives her to those who love Him.

Respecting the Lord brings honor, joy, and happiness. It is like a crown of celebration. It fills the heart with delight, brings gladness, and leads to a long life. Whoever fears the Lord will receive His favor, be blessed at the end of life, and be honored when it is time to leave this world.

Respect for the Lord is the beginning of wisdom. It is planted in the hearts of faithful people, even before they are born. Wisdom has built a strong foundation among humans, and her trust remains with their children. Respecting the Lord brings a life full of wisdom's gifts, and her rewards bring peace and contentment. She fills homes with treasures that are valuable and storerooms with blessings.

The fear of the Lord is the crown of wisdom. It brings peace and good health to all who follow her ways. The Lord measured wisdom and poured out knowledge and understanding. He gives honor to those who hold on to her. Respect for the Lord is the foundation of wisdom, and from it grows a long and fulfilling life.

Uncontrolled anger leads people to make mistakes and stumble. A patient person may struggle for a while, but joy will come in time. A wise person knows when to speak, and many will respect their words.

A wise saying is like a treasure kept safe with wisdom, but a sinner rejects what is good. If you want wisdom, follow the commandments, and the Lord will give it to you freely. Respect for the Lord brings wisdom and instruction, and He is pleased by faith and humility.

Do not turn away from the fear of the Lord, and do not approach Him with a divided heart. Do not pretend to be righteous in front of others if your heart is not sincere.

Be careful with your words. Do not lift yourself up too high, or you might fall and bring shame upon yourself. The Lord will reveal your secrets if you have not lived with true respect for Him. No dishonest heart can ever be hidden from Him.

Chapter 2

If you choose to serve the Lord, be ready to face challenges. Stay strong, be patient, and don't panic when trouble comes. Stay close to Him and don't turn away, so that in the end, you will be blessed. Accept any hardships that come your way, and stay patient when you feel brought down. Just like gold is purified in fire, people who are worthy are tested through struggles and suffering. Trust in Him, and He will support you. Follow the right path and put your hope in Him.

All of you who respect the Lord, wait for His mercy and don't turn away, or you will fall. Those who fear the Lord should trust Him, because your reward is guaranteed. Hope in the Lord for good things, eternal joy, and His mercy.

Look back at the stories of those who lived before you:

> Has anyone ever trusted in the Lord and been let down?
> Has anyone who stayed loyal to Him been left behind?
> Has anyone who called out to Him been ignored?

The Lord is full of kindness and mercy. He forgives sins and rescues people when they are in trouble.

But trouble will come to those who are fearful and weak, to those who hesitate between right and wrong. Trouble will also come to those who lack faith, because they won't be protected. And trouble will come to those who give up too soon—what will you do when the Lord comes to judge you?

Those who respect the Lord will follow His words. Those who love Him will live by His ways. Those who fear Him will try to please Him. Those who love Him will obey His commands. Those who fear the Lord will prepare their hearts and humble themselves before Him.

We choose to put our trust in the Lord rather than in people. His power is great, and so is His mercy.

Chapter 3

Listen to me, my children, as a father speaks to his family. Follow my advice so you can live safely. The Lord has given fathers respect over their children and given mothers authority over their sons. Whoever respects their father will have their sins forgiven, and whoever loves and honors their mother is like someone collecting valuable treasures. If you honor your father, you will find joy in your own children, and your prayers will be answered. Respecting your father will bring you a long life, and listening to the Lord will bring happiness to your mother.

Treat your parents with the same respect you would show a leader. Honor your father through your actions and words so that his blessing will be upon you. A father's blessing builds a strong foundation for his children's lives, but a mother's curse can bring them ruin. Do not take pride in your father's shame, because his dishonor does not bring honor to you. A person's dignity is tied to how they treat their father, and a mother's disgrace brings shame to her children.

Support your father as he grows older, and do not make his life difficult. Even if he starts to lose his understanding, be patient with him and do not disrespect him just because you feel stronger. The kindness you show your father will not be forgotten and will count in your favor instead of your mistakes. When you go through struggles, this kindness will be remembered, and your sins will disappear like frost melting in the sun. Abandoning your father is like rejecting God, and those who upset their mother will be judged by the Lord.

My child, live humbly, and you will be loved by those who are worthy. The more important you become, the more humble you should be, and the Lord will bless you. His power is beyond measure, and He is honored by those who live with humility.

Do not chase after things that are too hard for you to understand or try to figure out things beyond your ability. Focus on what the Lord has commanded, because you don't need to know everything. Do not worry about things that are too complicated, as God has already revealed more than you could ever fully understand. Pride has led many people to destruction, and their wrong beliefs have caused them to make foolish choices.

Just as you need eyes to see, you need knowledge to have wisdom. A stubborn heart will lead to trouble, and those who go looking for danger will eventually suffer because of it. A hard-hearted person will be weighed down by their struggles, and sinners will add more sins to their load. Prideful people cannot be healed because their wickedness has taken deep root.

A wise heart understands lessons, and a wise person values those who listen. Water can put out a burning fire, and helping others can make up for past mistakes. Those who give generously focus on what truly matters, and in their time of need, they will find help.

Chapter 4

My child, don't take away what a poor person needs to survive or make someone in need wait longer than necessary. Don't make a hungry person feel worse, and don't upset someone who is already struggling. Don't add to the pain of someone who is grieving, and don't delay when someone asks for your help. Never ignore someone who is suffering or turn your back on a poor person who comes to you. If someone asks for help, don't refuse them, and don't give anyone a reason to curse you. If a person cries out in frustration, God, who created them, will hear their prayer.

Respect your community and show humility to those in leadership. Listen to the poor and speak to them with kindness and patience. Help those who have been treated unfairly, and don't hesitate to stand for justice. Be like a father to orphans and a protector to widows, and you will be seen as a child of the Most High. He will love you even more than your own mother does.

Wisdom strengthens those who seek her and supports those who follow her. Whoever loves wisdom loves life, and those who search for her will find happiness. Staying close to wisdom brings honor, and the Lord will bless those who walk with her. Serving wisdom means serving the Holy One, and God loves those who love her. Those who listen to wisdom will have influence, and those who follow her will live in peace. If someone trusts in wisdom, they will inherit her, and their children will benefit from her as well.

At first, wisdom may lead a person through difficult times, testing their heart and challenging their soul with discipline. She will correct them and push them to grow. But once she sees that they are truly committed, she will guide them on the right path, bring joy into their life, and reveal her secrets to them. However, if they turn away from her, she will let them fall on their own.

Pay attention to opportunities and stay away from evil. Don't be ashamed to protect yourself. Some shame leads to sin, but other shame brings honor and kindness. Don't show favoritism to the wrong people, and don't lower yourself just because you are afraid of others. Speak up when necessary to protect yourself and others, and don't hide your wisdom to avoid upsetting people. A person's wisdom is shown by their words, and their knowledge is revealed by how they speak.

Don't go against the truth, or you will embarrass yourself with your ignorance. Don't be afraid to admit when you're wrong, and don't resist doing what is right. Don't let foolish people take advantage of you, and don't give special treatment to the powerful. Stand for the truth, even if it costs you everything, and the Lord will defend you.

Think before you speak, and don't be lazy in your actions. Don't act like a tyrant at home, and don't be overly suspicious of those who serve you. Don't be quick to take from others but slow to give back when it's time to repay.

Chapter 5

Do not depend on your wealth or say, "This is all I need." Do not follow your own desires or use your strength to chase after whatever your heart wants. Do not think, "No one can tell me what to do," because the Lord will hold you accountable.

Do not say, "I've done wrong, but nothing bad has happened," because the Lord is patient. Do not take forgiveness for granted and keep adding sin upon sin. Do not say, "God is always merciful, so He will forgive all my mistakes," because He is both merciful and just. His judgment will come upon those who continue to do wrong.

Do not wait to turn to the Lord. Do not keep putting it off, thinking you have plenty of time. His judgment could come suddenly, and you may be caught unprepared. Do not put your trust in dishonest wealth, because it will be useless when trouble comes.

Do not follow every new trend or go along with everything others do. That is the way of a dishonest person. Be firm in what you know is right, and let your words be thoughtful and trustworthy. Be quick to listen but slow to respond, speaking only after careful thought.

If you have wisdom, share it with your neighbor; but if you lack understanding, it is better to remain silent. Words have the power to bring either respect or disgrace, and a person's own speech can lead to their downfall.

Do not be known as someone who spreads gossip or uses words to hurt others. Just as a thief faces shame, those who speak dishonestly will face judgment.

Do not ignore anything, no matter how small or unimportant it may seem.

Chapter 6

Don't turn against others and become an enemy instead of a friend. A bad reputation brings shame and embarrassment, and those who lie or deceive will suffer because of it. Don't be arrogant or let your pride destroy you like a wild bull. Pride drains your strength, ruins your success, and leaves you empty like a dead tree. A wicked heart will slowly eat away at a person, making them a joke to their enemies.

Kind words help you make many friends, and showing respect earns admiration. Stay on good terms with many people, but only trust a few with your deepest secrets. If you want a real friend, test them in hard times before trusting them too quickly. Some people are only around when life is good but disappear when things go wrong. Others act friendly but later turn against you, causing trouble and shame.

Some people will gladly share your food and home, but when problems arise, they will leave you behind. When things are going well, they will act like they belong in your house, even ordering your servants around. But in bad times, they will betray you and disappear. Stay away from enemies, but even with friends, be cautious.

A true friend is like a strong shelter, as valuable as a rare treasure. No amount of money can buy a real friend because their worth is beyond measure. A loyal friend is like a healing medicine, and those who honor the Lord will find such a friend. People who fear the Lord will choose their friends wisely, because their friendships will reflect their character.

My child, seek wisdom early, and it will stay with you throughout your life. Search for wisdom like a farmer plants crops—be patient, and you will enjoy the harvest. The effort you put in will be small compared to the reward. To those who don't understand, wisdom may seem too difficult, and those who lack patience will give up on it. At first, wisdom may feel like a burden, but once you truly accept it, it will lead you to success.

Wisdom doesn't reveal herself to everyone, but she shows her true nature to those who seek her. Listen to me, my child, and follow my advice. Don't reject my guidance. Hold onto wisdom, even when it seems challenging at first. Be patient and don't resent the lessons she teaches. If you chase after wisdom with all your heart, she will show herself to you, and once you find her, never let her go.

In the end, wisdom will bring you peace and fill your heart with joy. Her lessons will strengthen you, and her guidance will bring honor to your life. Wisdom will be like a golden decoration and a royal robe, wrapping you in glory and happiness.

If you truly want to learn, you will. If you open your heart, wisdom will come to you. Love to listen, and you will gain knowledge. Pay close attention, and you will become wise. Spend time with elders and stay close to those who have wisdom. Listen eagerly to every good lesson, and don't ignore words of understanding. If you meet someone wise, seek them out early and visit them often.

Let your thoughts focus on the Lord's commandments, and reflect on His teachings. He will strengthen your heart, and your desire for wisdom will be fulfilled.

Chapter 7

Stay away from wrongdoing, and it will stay away from you. Turn away from evil, and it won't bother you. My child, don't plant the seeds of wickedness, or you'll harvest nothing but trouble. Don't demand greatness from the Lord or seek special honor from a king. Don't try to justify yourself before God, and don't show off your wisdom in front of powerful people.

Avoid becoming a judge if you're not ready for the responsibility, or you may struggle to correct injustices or let fear of the powerful influence your decisions. Don't sin against your community or bring shame upon yourself in public. Don't repeat your mistakes, because even one wrongdoing will be remembered. Don't think, "My many offerings will make up for my sins." Instead, come before God with a humble heart.

Don't be lazy in prayer, and always be generous to those in need. Never mock someone who is suffering, because the same God who humbles can also lift up. Don't lie about your brother or deceive your friend. Speak truthfully, because lies only bring harm. When you're among wise people, don't try to dominate the conversation, and when you pray, avoid meaningless repetition.

Respect hard work and farming, for they are part of God's plan. Don't surround yourself with sinners, remembering that God's judgment always comes in time. Be humble, for the wicked will face destruction. Don't trade a true friend for money or a loyal brother for wealth. Treasure a wise and kind wife, for her goodness is worth more than gold.

Treat a hardworking servant with fairness and kindness; don't take advantage of those who work for you. Value a wise servant, and if they prove themselves worthy, don't deny them their freedom. If you own animals, take good care of them; if they serve you well, be responsible for them. If you have children, teach and guide them early so they learn to be disciplined. Care for your daughters' well-being, but don't spoil them.

Choose a wise and good man for your daughter to marry, and you will have fulfilled an important duty. If you have a good wife, cherish her and don't push her away. But be cautious with those who show cruelty. Honor your parents with all your heart, and remember everything they have done for you. Think about how they raised you and brought you into this world, and consider how you can repay even a small part of their love and sacrifices.

Honor the Lord with all your heart, and show respect to His priests. Love your Creator with all your strength, and never turn your back on His servants. Fear God and give His priests their rightful share, including first fruits, offerings, and sacred gifts. Be generous to the poor so that your blessings will be complete.

Kindness and generosity bring favor, so don't hold back from helping others, even those who have passed away. Comfort those who are grieving and mourn with them. Don't hesitate to visit the sick, for these acts of kindness will build love and goodwill. In everything you do and say, keep eternity in mind, and you will avoid sin.

Chapter 8

Avoid arguing with someone in power, or you might end up under their control. Don't debate with a rich person, or they might use their wealth against you—money has led many people astray, even kings. Don't get into a fight with someone who loves to argue, and don't add to their anger—it's like adding wood to a fire.

Don't make fun of someone who has no respect for others, or you might bring shame to your own family. Don't judge someone who has changed their ways—remember, we all have made mistakes. Don't insult an elderly person, because one day you'll be old too. Don't celebrate when someone dies—death comes for everyone.

Don't ignore the wisdom of those who are experienced. Learn from their teachings—they will guide you and help you understand how to act around important people. Don't overlook the lessons of the elderly; they learned from those before them. Their words will help you grow in wisdom and teach you how to handle difficult situations.

Don't provoke a sinner, or you may get caught up in their anger. Don't challenge a rude person, or they may trap you with their words. Don't lend money to someone more powerful than you, but if you do, be ready to lose it.

Don't make promises you can't afford to keep, and if you do, be prepared to face the consequences. Don't take legal action against a judge, because the court will likely side with them out of respect for their position. Don't travel with a reckless person—they will only bring trouble. Their selfish and foolish behavior could put both of you in danger.

Don't fight with an angry person or go with them to dangerous places, because they don't value life. If trouble comes, they will abandon you and leave you to face it alone.

Don't seek advice from a fool—they won't know how to help you and won't keep your secrets. Don't share personal matters with a stranger—you never know what problems it could cause. Be careful not to open your heart to just anyone, and don't expect everyone to treat you with the same kindness you show them.

Chapter 9

Don't let jealousy take over when it comes to the wife you love, and don't teach her anything that could come back to harm you. Don't give your strength to a woman or let her control your life. Stay away from prostitutes, or you might fall into their trap. Avoid spending time with a woman who sings to entertain, as her charm could easily draw you in. Don't stare too long at a young woman, or you might get yourself into trouble. Don't give your heart to prostitutes, or you could lose everything you've worked hard for.

Don't wander the streets without a purpose or hang out in lonely places. Turn your eyes away from a beautiful woman, and don't focus too much on looks. Many have been led astray by beauty, as desire can burn quickly like fire. Don't eat or drink with a married woman, or you might start feeling attracted to her, leading to disaster.

Don't abandon an old friend because no new friend can fully replace them. A new friend is like fresh wine—it only brings real joy once it has aged. Don't be jealous of the success of sinful people, because you don't know how their lives will end. Don't take pleasure in the temporary happiness of the wicked. Remember, they won't escape judgment.

Stay far away from anyone who has the power to take a life, and you won't have to live in fear of death. If you must deal with such a person, be careful not to make a mistake that could cost you everything. Always remember that life is full of risks, like walking along the edge of a city wall.

Whenever you can, get to know your neighbors, and seek advice from wise people. Talk with those who understand what's right, and focus your conversations on the teachings of the Most High. Share your meals with good and righteous people, and let your true pride come from your respect for the Lord.

A skilled worker earns respect for their craft, just as a leader is honored for their wisdom. A loud and boastful person is a danger to their community, and someone who speaks carelessly will always be disliked.

Chapter 10

A wise judge teaches and guides his people, and a good leader keeps his government running smoothly. Just as a judge's character influences those he rules over, the way a leader governs affects the behavior of his people. A careless and reckless king can destroy his nation, but a wise ruler helps his city grow strong. It is the Lord who decides who rises and falls, placing leaders in power at the right time. True success comes from the Lord, who gives honor to those who seek wisdom, like a hardworking scribe.

Don't hold onto anger against your neighbor for every little mistake, and don't respond to others with violence. Both God and people dislike pride and arrogance. Nations lose their strength and fall apart because of injustice, greed, and cruelty. How can someone made from dust and ashes be proud, especially when our bodies start to decay even while we are still alive? Long illnesses remind us that even doctors have limits, and even the greatest kings today will face death tomorrow. In the end, all that remains of a person are bones, worms, and decay.

Pride begins when someone forgets about the Lord and turns away from the One who created them. It leads to sin, and those who hold onto it will bring trouble upon themselves. This is why the Lord has brought down the proud and removed them completely. He takes rulers off their thrones and replaces them with humble people. God uproots nations and replaces them with others. He tears down lands to their very foundations and wipes out some nations so completely that they are never remembered again.

Pride was never meant for people, and anger was not intended for human beings. Who deserves true honor? Those who respect the Lord. And who loses honor? Those who refuse to obey Him. In a family, the head of the household is respected, and those who fear the Lord are honored by Him. Both the rich and the poor find their greatest glory in respecting and worshiping the Lord. It is wrong to insult a wise poor person, just as it is wrong to praise someone who lives wickedly.

Princes, judges, and rulers may earn respect, but no one is greater than a person who fears the Lord. A wise servant will be honored, even among those who are free, and someone with knowledge won't complain about their situation. Don't brag about how smart you are while you work, and don't boast about your endurance during hard times. It is much better to work hard and have plenty than to be proud while struggling with hunger. My child, stay humble and only take credit for what you truly deserve.

How can you respect someone who brings harm to themselves? And how can honor be given to someone who treats their own life carelessly? A poor person can be respected for their wisdom, while a rich person is admired for their wealth. But if a poor person is honored, imagine how much greater their respect would be if they were wealthy. And if a rich person is disgraced, imagine how much worse their shame would be if they were poor.

Chapter 11

The wisdom of a humble person lifts them up and brings them into the company of important people. Don't admire someone just because they look good, and don't ignore someone just because of their appearance. Even though the bee is small compared to other flying creatures, it makes some of the sweetest honey. Don't brag about your clothes or take pride in awards, because the Lord's works are often amazing yet hidden from human eyes.

Many kings have been brought down and forced to sit on the ground, while those who were once ignored have been honored. Many powerful people have lost everything, and famous leaders have been given over to others. Don't judge anyone before you understand their situation. First, take the time to look into the matter, then offer your opinion. Don't answer before you've listened, and never interrupt someone when they are speaking. Stay away from arguments that don't involve you, and don't take sides with sinners in their disputes.

My child, don't take on too many tasks at once, or you'll end up making mistakes. If you chase after too much, you'll accomplish nothing, and avoiding problems won't guarantee you'll stay safe. Some people work endlessly but still fall behind, while others who seem weak and poor, with little strength, still manage to succeed. The Lord shows kindness to them, lifting them out of their struggles and surprising those who once looked down on them.

Both good and bad things, life and death, poverty and wealth—all come from the Lord. The blessings of the Lord remain with the righteous, and His gifts bring lasting success. Some people gain wealth through hard work and discipline, enjoying the rewards of their efforts, but in the end, they leave it all behind, never knowing how soon their time will come. Stay committed to your work, do it faithfully, and continue your efforts as you grow older.

Don't be jealous when sinners seem to succeed. Trust in the Lord and keep working hard, because God can turn a poor person into a wealthy one in an instant. His blessings can make the righteous successful overnight. Don't say, "There's nothing left for me," or, "What good can still happen to me?" Also, don't think, "I have everything I need, and nothing bad will ever happen to me." When people are happy, they forget their struggles, and when they face hardship, they forget the good times.

It's easy for the Lord to repay people for their actions when their lives come to an end. A single moment of suffering can erase years of happiness. In the end, a person's true character is revealed. Don't say someone is truly happy until their life is over, because their legacy is shown in how they are remembered and in the lives of their children.

Be careful about who you allow into your home, because some people are full of tricks and deceit. A proud person's heart is like a bird trapped in a cage, always looking for weaknesses, like a spy searching for an opportunity. They twist good things into bad and find faults even in things that deserve praise. A tiny spark can start a huge fire, and a sinful person waits for the right moment to harm others.

Stay away from those who do evil, because their schemes can ruin your reputation forever. If you let the wrong person into your home, they might create arguments and bring conflict into your family.

Chapter 12

When you choose to do good, be careful who you help so your kindness isn't wasted. Help those who live righteously, and you will be rewarded—if not by them, then by the Lord. But someone who constantly does wrong and refuses to give to others will not receive any blessings.

Give to those who do good, but don't support those who live in wickedness. Help those in need, but don't assist the ungodly. Don't give them food or resources, or they might turn against you, and later, you'll regret helping them. The Lord despises those who do evil and will bring judgment upon them. Do good to the righteous, but don't encourage the wicked.

A friend's loyalty isn't tested when life is easy, and an enemy can't stay hidden when trouble comes. When someone is successful, their enemies will resent them, and when they struggle, even their friends might leave them. Never put your trust in an enemy, because their wickedness is as persistent as rust on metal.

Even if your enemy pretends to be humble and acts like they have changed, be cautious. They may seem harmless for a while, but their true nature will show eventually. Don't let them stand beside you, or they might push you aside and take your place. Don't put them in a position of power, or they will try to take what's yours. When that happens, you'll remember this advice and regret not listening to it.

No one feels sorry for a snake charmer who gets bitten by a snake or for someone who approaches a wild animal and gets attacked. In the same way, no one will pity you if you choose to associate with a sinner and end up suffering because of it. A sinner may stay close to you for a while, but when trouble comes, they will leave without hesitation.

Your enemy might speak kindly and use flattering words, but in his heart, he is planning your downfall. He may even shed tears to seem sincere, but if given the chance, he will hurt you worse than before. When you face difficulties, he will be there—not to help you, but to take advantage of your weakness. He might act like he's offering support, but his real goal is to make you fail. He will mock you with his actions, whisper behind your back, and his true nature will be revealed in the way he looks at you and treats you.

Chapter 13

Anyone who touches tar will get sticky, and anyone who spends time with arrogant people will start acting like them. Don't take on more than you can handle, and don't try to be close to someone much stronger or richer than you. A fragile clay pot can't be friends with a sturdy metal kettle—if they collide, the clay pot will break.

A rich person can do wrong and still act tough, but a poor person, even when wronged, will have to apologize. If you are useful to a wealthy person, he will take advantage of you, but if you ever need help, he will turn his back on you. As long as you have something he wants, he'll stick around, but once he's taken all he can, he won't feel bad about leaving you empty-handed.

When he needs something from you, he'll act friendly and make you think he cares. He'll smile, pretend to be generous, and ask, "What do you need?" But behind the scenes, he's planning how to take more from you than you ever expected. Once he's done using you, he'll laugh at you, walk away without a second thought, and never feel guilty.

Be careful not to let yourself be fooled while trying to enjoy life. If a powerful person invites you somewhere, act humbly, and you may be invited back. But don't try too hard to impress him, or he'll push you away. At the same time, don't act too distant, or he might forget about you completely.

Don't assume you're on the same level as him, and don't believe everything he says. He may flatter you to see how you respond, but he's really watching you closely. A person who can't keep a secret can't be trusted. When the time is right, he won't hesitate to harm you or take advantage of you.

Keep your thoughts to yourself and be careful what you say, because you're walking on uncertain and dangerous ground.

Chapter 14

Every creature is drawn to its own kind, and people naturally connect with those who are similar to them. Each being stays with its group, and humans are no different. A wolf cannot be friends with a lamb, just as sinners and the godly cannot truly get along. A hyena and a dog don't live together peacefully, just like the rich and the poor often find themselves in conflict.

Lions hunt wild donkeys in the wilderness, and in the same way, the wealthy take advantage of the poor. A proud person looks down on those who are humble, just as a rich person often despises the poor. When a wealthy person faces trouble, they have plenty of supporters, but when a poor person struggles, even their friends turn away. If a rich person fails, many people will come to their aid and defend them, even if they are wrong. But if a poor person makes a mistake, they are criticized, and even when they speak wisely, no one listens.

When a rich person speaks, people fall silent and praise their words. But if a poor person tries to speak, others ignore them and say, "Who is this?" If they make a small mistake, people push them down even further.

Wealth is a gift when it comes without wrongdoing, but the ungodly see poverty as something shameful.

A person's heart is reflected in their face—whether they feel joy or sorrow. A cheerful face shows a happy heart, but wise thoughts require deep reflection. Blessed is the one who speaks with wisdom and avoids suffering caused by their own sins. Happy is the person whose heart is at peace and who holds onto hope.

Wealth is wasted on those who hoard it—what good is money if they never use it? A miser saves by denying themselves happiness, only for others to enjoy what they've gathered after they're gone. If someone doesn't treat themselves well, how can they be kind to others? They don't even enjoy their own possessions.

No one is more miserable than a person who refuses to enjoy life—that's their punishment for being greedy. Even when they do something good, they quickly forget it, and in the end, their selfishness is clear. A miser is harsh and turns away from those in need. Greedy people are never satisfied with what they have because their selfishness eats away at them. They even begrudge the bread on their own table.

My child, enjoy the good things you have and honor the Lord with your offerings. Remember, death comes when you least expect it. Be generous to your friends while you can, and share as much as you are able. Don't let life's pleasures pass you by or let your desires slip through your fingers. In the end, everything you worked for will belong to someone else. What you've earned will be divided among others when you're gone.

So enjoy life, give freely, and receive with gratitude, because there are no luxuries in the grave. Life is like the leaves on a tree—some fall, and others grow. Generations come and go, just like the seasons. Every effort fades, and its maker leaves with it.

Blessed is the one who reflects on wisdom and lets understanding shape their thoughts. Those who carefully seek wisdom will uncover her secrets. Chase after her like a hunter and be patient as her path unfolds. Look through her windows and listen at her doors. Stay close to her home and secure yourself to her firmly.

Make your home near her and rest in the goodness she brings. Let her shelter your children and provide shade for them under her branches. She will protect you from life's hardships and cover you with her beauty.

Chapter 15

Those who respect the Lord will follow His ways, and those who stay committed to His teachings will find wisdom. Wisdom will come to them like a caring mother and hold them close like a loving bride. She will nourish them with understanding and give them the refreshing water of wisdom to drink.

They will rely on her and remain steady. They will trust in her and never feel ashamed. Wisdom will lift them up above others and give them the confidence to speak in public. They will receive joy, honor, and a lasting reputation.

Foolish people cannot understand wisdom, and sinners cannot even recognize her. She stays far away from the arrogant, and liars quickly forget about her. Praise does not belong in the mouths of sinners, for the Lord does not allow them to have it. True praise comes from wisdom, and the Lord makes sure it continues.

Do not say, "The Lord made me do wrong," because He never leads anyone toward what He hates. Do not claim, "He caused me to sin," because the Lord has no use for those who choose evil. He despises all wickedness, and those who respect Him will turn away from it.

From the very beginning, He created people and gave them the freedom to choose their own path. If you truly want to, you can follow His commandments—it's completely up to you. He has placed fire and water before you, and you are free to choose either one.

Life and death are in front of every person, and they will receive whichever one they reach for. The Lord's wisdom is beyond understanding. He is all-powerful and sees everything. His eyes are always watching over those who honor Him, and He knows all of their actions.

The Lord has never told anyone to do evil, and He has never given permission for anyone to sin.

Chapter 16

Do not wish for many children if they will not live righteously, and do not be proud of ungodly offspring. If your children grow in number, do not rejoice unless they respect the Lord. Do not place your hopes in them simply because they are many, for one righteous child is better than a thousand, and it is better to have no children than to raise those who turn away from God.

A single wise person can restore a city, but a group of wicked people will bring it to ruin. I have seen these truths with my own eyes and heard of even greater ones. Among sinners, the fire of judgment will burn, and in nations that reject God, His wrath will be unleashed.

God did not spare the mighty giants of ancient times who became proud and rebelled. He showed no mercy to the arrogant people of Sodom, whom He despised for their pride. He did not pity those who perished in their sins, nor did He spare the six hundred thousand soldiers who hardened their hearts against Him. Even one stubborn person rarely escapes punishment, for God is both merciful and just. He forgives, but He also brings judgment.

His mercy is as great as His discipline, and He judges everyone according to their actions. A sinner will not get away with what they have taken, and the perseverance of the righteous will not be ignored. God rewards every good deed and repays everyone according to what they deserve.

Do not say, "The Lord does not see me," or, "I am just one person among many, and He will forget me." Do not think, "What does my life matter compared to all of creation?" Look at the heavens, the deep oceans, and the earth—they all tremble at His presence. The mountains shake, and the foundations of the world quake when He looks at them. No human mind can fully understand these things, for who can truly comprehend His ways?

Most of His works remain hidden, like a storm before it appears. Who can declare all His acts of righteousness or fully understand His promises that seem far off? Only a foolish and unwise person refuses to see these truths.

My child, listen to me and learn wisdom. Pay attention to my words and let them guide your heart. I will teach you carefully and provide knowledge with accuracy.

God's works were set in place from the beginning, and He established their purpose when creation began.

He arranged everything for all time and determined how each generation would unfold. His creations do not grow tired or stop working, and no one can interfere with the order He has commanded. They obey His word without hesitation.

Then, the Lord looked upon the earth and blessed it richly. He filled its surface with all kinds of living creatures, and in time, they return to the earth from which they came.

Chapter 17

The Lord created humans from the earth, and one day, they will return to it. He decided how long they would live and gave them control over everything on the earth. He made them strong according to their nature and formed them in His own image. He placed fear of humans in all living creatures and gave people authority over animals and birds.

He gave humans the ability to think, speak, see, hear, and understand. He filled their minds with wisdom and taught them to recognize right from wrong. He placed His attention on their hearts and showed them the wonders of His creations.

They were made to honor His holy name and speak of His greatness. He gave them knowledge and entrusted them with His teachings as a lasting gift. He made an everlasting covenant with them and revealed His commandments. They witnessed His glory and heard the power of His voice.

He instructed them to stay away from evil and taught them how to treat one another with fairness. Their actions are always seen by Him, and nothing is hidden from His sight.

He appointed leaders over every nation, but Israel remains His chosen people.

Chapter 18

Everything people do is as clear as day to the Lord, and He always watches the paths they take. Nothing is hidden from Him, and all their sins are completely visible to Him.

The Lord values acts of kindness like a precious seal, and He treasures mercy as something incredibly important. At the right time, He will repay everyone for what they have done, returning their actions to them. But for those who turn back to Him, He offers forgiveness and brings comfort to those who feel hopeless.

Turn back to the Lord and leave your sins behind. Pray to Him and stop doing what offends Him. Return to the Most High and give up your wrongdoing. Hate what is evil. Who can praise the Lord from the grave? Only the living can give thanks. The dead cannot express gratitude, just as someone who no longer exists cannot honor Him. It is the living, those who still have breath and strength, who can glorify the Lord.

The Lord's mercy is endless, and He forgives those who repent and come back to Him. People have limits, and no one lives forever. Even the bright sun can be covered by an eclipse, and human nature often leads to mistakes. The Lord watches over everything from the heights of heaven, but to Him, people are like dust and ashes.

The eternal Lord created everything. He alone is truly righteous and just. No one can fully explain His works, nor can anyone completely understand His mighty deeds. Who can measure the power of His glory? Who can grasp the depth of His mercy? His wonders cannot be added to or taken away, and no one can fully understand them. When someone thinks they have figured it all out, they are only at the beginning. When they stop searching, they are left in awe.

What are people, and what purpose do we serve? What good do we bring, and what harm do we cause? Even at best, human life is short—just a tiny drop in the vast ocean of time or a small pebble compared to eternity. Because of this, the Lord is patient with people and pours out His mercy. He sees their struggles and increases His forgiveness toward them.

People can only show kindness to those around them, but the Lord's mercy extends to everyone. He corrects, teaches, and guides people like a shepherd leading his sheep. He is compassionate toward those who accept His discipline and choose to follow His ways.

My child, don't ruin your good deeds with harsh words or criticism when helping others. Just as dew cools the heat, a kind word is better than any gift. A kind word can be more valuable than a present, and both come naturally from a generous heart.

A foolish person is rude and ungrateful, while a stingy person gives with bitterness, leaving others feeling discouraged. Learn before you speak, and take care of your health before you get sick. Reflect on yourself before judging others, and you may find mercy when you are the one being judged. Humble yourself before trouble comes, and when you make mistakes, turn back and make things right.

Don't delay in keeping your promises, and don't wait until the end of your life to free yourself from your obligations. Think carefully before making commitments, and don't act as if you are testing the Lord. Remember that consequences can come at the end of life and that judgment may arrive when you least expect it. In good times, remember the days when you struggled. During times of success, think back to moments of hardship.

Life can change quickly—from morning to evening, everything can shift in an instant before the Lord. A wise person is careful in all things and avoids falling into sin. Those who have understanding seek wisdom and are grateful when they find it. Those who learn the meaning of wise sayings grow wiser and share meaningful words with others.

Don't give in to every desire, and keep your cravings under control. If you let your desires control you, they will make you a joke to your enemies. Avoid overindulging in luxury, and don't let it become a burden. Don't end up begging because you spent all your money on extravagant feasts and pleasures when you have nothing left.

Chapter 19

A worker who spends too much time drinking will never become rich. Someone who ignores small responsibilities will eventually lose everything. Both alcohol and unhealthy relationships can mislead even the smartest people, and anyone who wastes their time with unfaithful partners is acting foolishly. A person like that will end up with nothing but regret and shame, and their reckless lifestyle will destroy them.

Trusting others too quickly is not wise, and those who keep making bad choices only hurt themselves. Enjoying wrongdoing will lead to judgment, but avoiding gossip will help you stay out of trouble.

If you can keep a secret, people will trust you. Whether the information comes from a friend or an enemy, keep it to yourself unless staying silent would cause harm. If people find out you have spread their secrets, they may come to dislike you. If someone tells you something in confidence, respect their trust. Staying quiet takes self-control, but it won't hurt you to do so.

A fool finds it hard to keep a secret, like a woman struggling in childbirth. Gossiping is as painful to a fool as a thorn stuck deep in the skin. If you suspect your friend of wrongdoing, ask them—it's possible they didn't do it, or if they did, they might decide not to do it again. In the same way, if you think your neighbor said something harmful, talk to them about it. They may not have said it, or they may be more careful about their words in the future.

Be cautious in your friendships because gossip and slander are common. Don't believe everything you hear. People make mistakes, but often they don't mean to. Who hasn't, at some point, said something foolish? If someone wrongs you, correct them kindly before getting angry, and let God's laws guide your actions.

True wisdom begins with respecting the Lord. Following His commandments is where wisdom is found. Any knowledge that is used to do harm is not real wisdom. The ideas of those who love sin will only lead to bad decisions and disaster. Some things are truly disgraceful, and some people completely lack understanding.

It is better to know a little but have a deep respect for God than to be highly intelligent while ignoring His ways. Some people use their cleverness unfairly, twisting the truth to get what they want. Others pretend to be humble, lowering their heads and acting modestly, but inside, they are full of deceit. They may appear harmless, but if given the chance, they will take advantage of you. If they don't have the power to act on their selfish plans right away, they will wait patiently for the right moment.

A person's character can often be seen in their appearance. Someone with wisdom can often be recognized by their expression. The way a person dresses, their laughter, and even how they carry themselves say a lot about who they really are.

Chapter 20

Sometimes, it's better to stay silent than to correct someone. Giving advice calmly is more effective than reacting in anger. Admitting when you're wrong can help prevent bigger problems.

The desire of someone unable to marry for a bride is as pointless as trying to force justice through violence. Some people are respected for being quiet, while others are disliked for talking too much. Some stay silent because they have nothing important to say, while others know that silence is sometimes the best choice. A wise person speaks at the right moment, but a fool talks nonstop and misses opportunities. Talking too much can lead to resentment, and those who take power selfishly will face opposition.

Sometimes, bad luck can turn into success, while success can lead to trouble. Some gifts have no real benefit, while others bring even greater rewards. Fame can sometimes lead to downfall, while those who start with nothing may rise to greatness. Some people make small choices that lead to huge losses in the long run.

A wise person is admired for their words, but foolish jokes have no meaning. Gifts from a fool are useless because they come with expectations. A fool gives sparingly but expects endless praise, boasting about their generosity. They lend today and demand repayment tomorrow, making them difficult to be around.

A fool complains, "I have no friends, and no one appreciates my kindness. Even those who eat my food talk behind my back." People like this become the target of jokes and gossip. It is better to trip on a rock than to stumble with your words because once a fool messes up, their downfall is quick.

A story told at the wrong time by someone who lacks grace becomes a joke among those who don't understand. When a fool shares a wise saying, people ignore it because it's shared in the wrong way. Some people avoid sin, not because they are good, but because they don't have the opportunity to do wrong. They rest without worries. Others ruin their own lives with foolish decisions, breaking promises and turning friends into enemies for no reason.

A lie damages a person's reputation, and foolish people will keep repeating it. A thief is less shameful than a constant liar, but both will eventually face destruction. A liar's disgrace never goes away, and their shame follows them forever. Wise words lead to success, and those with understanding earn the respect of important people.

A hardworking farmer enjoys a good harvest, and those who earn the favor of leaders may have their mistakes overlooked. Bribes and gifts can influence even the wisest person, silencing criticism like a muzzle stops a voice.

Wisdom that is hidden, like a treasure that is never found, is useless. It's better to keep your foolishness hidden than to hide your wisdom.

Chapter 21

If you've done something wrong, my child, don't do it again. Instead, ask for forgiveness and turn away from it. Stay far from sin, just like you would avoid a poisonous snake—if you get too close, it will attack. Its bite is deadly, like a lion's, and it can destroy lives. Sin is like a sharp sword that cuts deep, leaving wounds that never fully heal.

Wealth can disappear because of fear and violence, and arrogance will lead to destruction. The prayers of the poor reach God, and He responds quickly with justice. Those who reject correction follow the path of sinners, but those who respect the Lord feel regret and change their ways.

Someone who speaks boldly may become famous, but a truly wise person recognizes their own mistakes. Building a house with stolen money is like digging your own grave. A group of wicked people is like dry straw, ready to catch fire. A sinner's path may seem easy at first, but it leads to disaster.

Those who follow God's law understand its purpose, and true wisdom starts with respecting Him. A person who lacks understanding resists learning, and even intelligence can turn into foolishness without proper guidance. Wisdom flows like a river from the heart of a wise person, and their words bring life to others.

A fool's mind is like a broken jar—it can't hold wisdom. A wise person hears good advice and values it, making it even more useful, but a careless person hears the same advice and ignores it. A fool's constant talking creates problems, while wise words bring peace.

A thoughtful person's words are treasured in conversations, and people remember what they say. But to a fool, wisdom feels like a collapsing house, and their understanding is nothing but meaningless chatter. A fool sees discipline as a punishment, something they want to escape.

A fool laughs loudly without reason, while a wise person smiles with quiet control. To the wise, learning is like a valuable piece of jewelry that makes them better. A fool rushes into a house without thinking, but an experienced person approaches carefully. A fool peeks inside without shame, while a respectful person waits patiently.

Eavesdropping is rude and disrespectful, but a wise person avoids this kind of behavior. It offends others, while the wise choose their words carefully. A fool speaks without thinking, letting their thoughts spill out, but wise people speak only after careful reflection.

When a wicked person curses someone else, the curse often comes back to them. Someone who spreads gossip brings shame on themselves and is disliked wherever they go.

Chapter 22

A lazy person is like a dirty rock that people laugh at in disgust. He is also like a pile of garbage—anyone who touches him will quickly shake him off.

A rebellious child brings shame to his father, and a foolish daughter causes him deep sadness. A wise daughter will find a good husband, but a disrespectful one brings pain to her father. A proud and arrogant daughter embarrasses both her father and husband, and they will grow to resent her.

Speaking at the wrong time is like playing cheerful music at a funeral—it doesn't fit. But correction and discipline bring wisdom in every situation. Teaching a fool is as pointless as trying to glue together broken pottery or waking someone who is deeply asleep. Trying to explain something to them is like talking to someone who is half-asleep—they'll just ask, "What are you talking about?"

Mourn for the dead because they have lost their life, but mourn even more for a fool because they lack understanding. It's better to grieve for the dead because they are at peace, while a fool's life is filled with misery.

Mourning for the dead lasts seven days, but dealing with a fool or a wicked person can bring sorrow for a lifetime.

Don't waste your time talking to a fool, and don't spend too much time with those who lack sense. Stay away from them, or you'll get caught up in their troubles and foolishness. Walk away, and you'll find peace, free from their nonsense.

What is heavier than lead? Dealing with a fool. Carrying a heavy load of sand, salt, or iron is easier than dealing with someone who refuses to understand.

Wood that is tightly fastened won't come loose, and a heart that is filled with wisdom will stay steady. A strong mind full of understanding is like smooth plaster on a solid wall—it won't crumble easily.

Fences built on a hill can't stand against strong winds, just like the weak thoughts of a coward will collapse at the first sign of fear. If you poke someone in the eye, they will cry, and if you hurt someone's heart, their emotions will show. Throwing a stone at birds will make them scatter, and insulting a friend can destroy a relationship.

If you have argued with a friend, don't lose hope— peace may still be possible. If you have spoken harshly to them, don't give up—things might still be fixed unless you have insulted them, acted with pride, shared their secrets, or betrayed them. Those things will end any friendship.

Stay loyal to your friend during hard times so you can celebrate with them when things get better. Stand by them when they struggle, and you may share in their success when they rise.

Just as smoke and steam appear before a fire, insults often lead to conflict. I will never hesitate to stand up for a friend or turn away when they need my help. Even if I suffer because of my loyalty, others will learn from my example.

Who will help me control my words and give me wisdom in what I say? I need guidance to avoid making mistakes or ruining myself with careless speech.

Chapter 23

O Lord, my Father and Master of my life, don't let me follow bad advice or make mistakes that lead me to trouble. Teach me discipline and place wisdom in my heart so I don't excuse my wrongs or fail to see my own faults. If I ignore them, my sins will only grow, and I may fall, giving my enemies a reason to celebrate my downfall.

O Lord, my Father and God of my life, protect me from arrogance and pride. Keep me from selfish desires, and don't let greed or lust control me. Do not leave me to a reckless and shameless mind.

Listen, my children, to the wisdom of controlling your words. Those who guard their speech avoid falling into traps. A sinner is destroyed by their own words, and the proud are brought down by their boasting. Do not let yourself get used to swearing, and do not take the Lord's Name lightly. Just like a servant who is often beaten carries scars, a person who swears carelessly will never be free from guilt.

Someone who swears without thinking fills their life with sin, and trouble will follow them. If they sin, they are to blame. If they ignore their mistakes, they only make things worse. If they lie under oath, they won't escape judgment, and their home will suffer because of it.

There are words that bring death. Let such speech never be found among God's people. Those who follow the Lord avoid such sin. Do not let crude or offensive language become a habit, for it leads to further wrongdoing.

When you sit among wise and respected people, remember your parents and their teachings. Do not act foolishly or forget their guidance, because bad habits will embarrass you and make you regret your actions. Someone who constantly speaks harshly will never change, no matter how long they live.

There are two types of people who increase sin, and a third who invites God's anger. Lust is like a fire that destroys everything in its path. A person who is ruled by desire will never be satisfied until it ruins them.

To someone controlled by lust, every opportunity to sin seems tempting, and they will not stop until their actions lead to disaster. A man who is unfaithful to his wife thinks, "No one sees me. The darkness hides me, and the walls protect me. No one will find out. Who do I have to fear? Surely God won't remember my sins."

This man worries about being judged by people but forgets that the Lord sees everything. His eyes are brighter than the sun, watching every path and uncovering every hidden place. The Lord has seen all things since the beginning and continues to witness every action. This man will be punished in the open, and his downfall will come when he least expects it.

The same is true for a wife who leaves her husband and has children with another man. First, she disobeyed God's law. Second, she betrayed her husband. Third, she committed adultery and bore children from another man. She will face judgment before her community, and her shame will affect her family.

Her children will not prosper, her family line will fade, and she will leave no lasting legacy. Her name will serve as a warning, and her disgrace will never be forgotten. Those who witness her downfall will understand that nothing is greater than fearing the Lord and nothing is better than obeying His commandments.

Chapter 24

Wisdom speaks with pride and declares her greatness among her people. She makes her voice heard in the assembly of the Most High and reveals her glory in His presence.

"I came from the mouth of the Most High and spread across the earth like a mist. I lived in the highest places, and my throne stood in a pillar of cloud. I traveled alone through the heavens and walked through the deep waters below. I ruled over the waves of the sea, the earth, and every nation and people.

I searched for a place to rest and asked where I should settle. Then the Creator of all things gave me a command. The One who made me decided that I should dwell in Jacob and make Israel my home. He created me before time began, and I will remain forever.

I served before Him in the holy tabernacle, and He placed me in Zion. He gave me a resting place in His beloved city, and Jerusalem became my home. I took root among His chosen people, in the land given to the Lord.

I grew tall like a cedar in Lebanon and like a cypress on Mount Hermon. I flourished like a palm tree by the seashore and like the rose bushes of Jericho. I became as beautiful as an olive tree in the plains and as strong as a great tree in the city squares.

I gave off a sweet fragrance like cinnamon and balsam. My scent was like the finest myrrh, like galbanum, onycha, stacte, and frankincense in the holy tabernacle. I spread my branches like a mighty oak, showing both beauty and grace.

I blossomed like a vine, and my flowers bore rich and abundant fruit.

"Come to me, all who desire wisdom, and be filled with my fruits. My memory is sweeter than honey, and my inheritance is more delightful than the honeycomb. Those who partake of me will always want more, and those who drink of me will thirst for more. Whoever follows me will never be ashamed, and those who work with me will not fall into sin."

All of these teachings are found in the book of the covenant of the Most High, the law that Moses gave as an inheritance to the people of Jacob.

Wisdom flows like the Pishon and Tigris rivers in the early harvest. Understanding is as plentiful as the waters of the Euphrates and Jordan during the time of gathering. Instruction shines as brightly as light, like the Gihon River during the grape harvest.

No one has fully grasped wisdom at the beginning, and no one will completely understand her at the end. Her thoughts are as vast as the ocean, and her counsel is as deep as the great waters.

I flowed like a canal from a river, like an irrigation stream into a garden. I said, "I will water my plants and drench their roots." Suddenly, my stream became a river, and my river swelled into a sea.

I will continue to shine wisdom like the morning sun and make knowledge clear from afar. I will pour out teachings like prophecy and leave them for all future generations.

Understand that my work is not for myself alone but for all who truly seek wisdom."

Chapter 25

I find joy in three things that are beautiful to both God and people: family members living in harmony, neighbors treating each other with kindness, and a husband and wife supporting each other with love. But there are three types of people I can't stand, and their behavior deeply bothers me: a poor man who is arrogant, a rich man who lies, and an old man who foolishly chases after sinful desires.

If you don't save or plan wisely when you're young, how can you expect to have anything when you're old? It's a wonderful thing when older people have good judgment, and it's a blessing when elders share their wisdom and give thoughtful advice. The wisdom of older men is valuable, and the understanding of respected elders is priceless. Their experience is like a crown of honor, and their greatest achievement is their deep respect for God.

There are nine things I have thought about, and in my heart, I see them as blessings. The tenth, I will now say out loud: a man who finds joy in his children and someone who lives to see his enemies defeated. Blessed is the man who has a wise wife, who speaks carefully and avoids careless words, and who has never been forced to serve an unworthy person. Happy is the one who makes good decisions and speaks wisely to those who listen. Wisdom is a great gift, but no one is greater than the person who deeply respects God. Respect for the Lord is the most important thing. Who can compare to someone who truly honors Him?

Nothing is harder to bear than a broken heart. No wickedness is worse than the cruelty of a bad woman. No disaster feels heavier than betrayal by those who hate you. No revenge is more painful than that of an enemy. There is no poison more dangerous than a snake's bite, and no anger worse than an enemy's rage.

I would rather live with a lion or a dragon than share a home with an evil woman. Her wickedness shows even on her face, making her expression as dark and frightening as a bear's. Her husband will sit with his neighbors, sighing in sorrow when he hears them whispering about her. There is no wickedness worse than what a bad woman can do. A woman like that is truly a punishment meant for sinners.

Living with a nagging wife is as tiring for a quiet man as climbing a steep hill is for an elderly person. Don't be fooled by a woman's beauty, and don't desire her just for her looks. If a woman takes over her husband's role as the provider, it leads to arguments, disrespect, and shame. A bad wife brings pain to her husband's heart, sadness to his face, and deep sorrow to his soul. A wife who doesn't bring joy to her husband is like weak hands or unsteady knees that cannot hold him up.

Sin entered the world through a woman, and because of that, we all face death. Don't let water spill where it shouldn't, and don't let a wicked woman say whatever she wants without control. If she refuses to listen to reason, it's better to separate from her completely.

Chapter 26

A man with a good wife is truly fortunate. His life will feel as if his days are twice as long. A loving and faithful wife brings happiness to her husband, and he will enjoy his years in peace. A good wife is a wonderful gift, given to those who respect and honor the Lord. No matter if a man is rich or poor, a kind and loving wife will always bring joy to his heart.

There are three things that make me afraid, and for the fourth, I pray: false rumors spreading through a city, a violent mob coming together, and being wrongly accused. These things are worse than death. A jealous wife brings sorrow and pain; her harsh words make her anger obvious to everyone. A wicked wife is like a heavy burden, and living with her is as risky as grabbing a scorpion. A wife who drinks too much causes shame and embarrassment, and she cannot hide her disgrace.

You can tell if a woman is unfaithful by the way she looks at others; her eyes reveal her intentions. Watch over a strong-willed daughter so she doesn't take advantage of her freedom and act recklessly. Be cautious of an inappropriate glance, and don't be surprised if it leads to trouble. She will be like a thirsty traveler drinking from any stream she finds. She will sit on every street corner, accepting anyone without restraint.

A good wife brings happiness to her husband, and her wisdom makes him stronger. A quiet and gentle woman is a gift from the Lord, and nothing is as valuable as a well-guided heart. A modest wife is a blessing beyond measure; her self-control is worth more than any treasure. The beauty of a good wife shines in her well-kept home, like the sunrise in the sky. Just as a beautiful face looks best on a balanced body, a graceful and faithful woman is like a lamp that brightens a sacred space. A woman with steady feet and a strong heart is like golden pillars set on a silver base.

There are two things that deeply trouble me, and a third that fills me with anger: a warrior who struggles with poverty, wise men who are treated as worthless, and someone who abandons righteousness to return to sin. The Lord will prepare such a person for judgment. It is hard for a merchant to stay completely honest, and a shopkeeper must work hard to avoid sin.

Chapter 27

Many people make bad choices when they are obsessed with getting rich. Someone desperate for wealth often ignores what is right and wrong. Just as a nail holds two stones together, sin is often mixed into business dealings. Without a strong foundation in respect for the Lord, a household will quickly fall apart.

When you shake a sieve, the unwanted bits are left behind. In the same way, a person's weaknesses are revealed through their thoughts. A potter tests his pottery in fire, and a person's true nature is shown by what's in their heart. Just like a tree's health is known by its fruit, a person's words reveal the condition of their soul. Don't be too quick to praise someone—listen to their thoughts first. Their words will show you who they really are.

If you seek righteousness, you will find it, and it will become part of you like a beautiful robe. Birds stay with their own kind, and truth gathers around those who live by it. Just as a lion waits to attack its prey, sin lies in wait for those who wander from the right path.

A wise person speaks carefully, but a fool is as unpredictable as the changing moon. Stay away from people who lack understanding and instead surround yourself with thoughtful, wise individuals. The way fools talk is offensive; their laughter is wild and full of sin. Their loud, disrespectful words make others avoid them, and their constant arguing frustrates those around them. Proud people start fights that can quickly turn violent, and their insults can deeply wound others.

Someone who can't keep a secret will ruin friendships and never gain trust. Stay loyal to your friends and protect their private matters. If you betray them, you might as well be an enemy. Losing a friend is like letting a bird fly out of your hand—you won't be able to catch it again. Don't chase after them; they'll be as impossible to reach as a deer running from danger.

Wounds can heal, and arguments can be solved, but revealing someone's secrets causes lasting damage. A person who winks while talking is usually up to no good, and those who notice it will stay away from them. They may say nice things to your face, but later, they twist your words and use them against you. I dislike many things, but this kind of behavior is the worst—and God hates it too.

Anyone who throws a stone straight up will have it fall back on their own head. A person who attacks others unfairly will end up getting hurt. Those who dig a pit to trap someone will fall into it themselves. Evil always finds its way back to the person who does it, often when they least expect it.

Proud people use insults and mockery to hurt others, but judgment is waiting for them like a lion ready to attack. Those who enjoy watching good people fail will end up trapped by their own schemes. Their lives will be filled with misery before they come to an end. Anger and hatred destroy people, and only those who refuse to change will hold on to them.

Chapter 28

Those who seek revenge will face God's judgment, and He will hold them accountable for their own sins. If you forgive others for their mistakes, God will forgive you when you ask for mercy. How can someone hold a grudge and still expect the Lord to heal them? If a person refuses to show kindness to others, how can they expect kindness for themselves?

If you cling to anger, who will stand up for you when you need forgiveness? Think about how short life is and let go of hate. Remember that one day, everyone returns to dust, so stay focused on following God's commands. Keep His teachings in your heart and don't hold grudges. Instead, remember the agreement made with the Most High and forgive those who acted out of ignorance.

Avoid conflict, and you will avoid sin. An angry person creates division, and a troublemaker ruins friendships and peace between neighbors. Just as a fire grows when fed with wood, an argument grows when fueled by strong emotions. The greater the anger, the bigger the damage. A person's temper often matches their power, and their wealth can make them even more aggressive.

Jumping into an argument is like lighting a match—it can quickly turn into a disaster. If you blow on a spark, it will grow into flames, but if you spit on it, it will go out. The choice is yours. Curse those who spread gossip and lies because they have ruined the lives of many.

Lies and slander have forced people to flee their homes, destroyed cities, and brought down leaders. They have driven strong women away from what they worked hard to earn. Those who believe gossip will never have peace or live a quiet life.

A whip leaves marks on the body, but hurtful words can break a person's spirit. While many have died from weapons, even more have been destroyed by cruel words. Blessed are those who have never suffered because of slander, who have never carried its burden or felt its weight.

Slander is heavier than iron and stronger than chains. Its impact can feel worse than death itself. But those who live righteously will not be overcome by it. It cannot burn them or bring them down. However, those who turn away from God will be destroyed by it. Gossip and lies will devour them like a roaring lion or a wild leopard ready to tear them apart.

Just as you carefully guard your valuables, you should also guard your words. Lock your mouth like a door with a strong key. Be careful what you say, or you

Translated by Tim Zengerink

may fall into the hands of those waiting to use your words against you.

Chapter 29

Those who are kind and generous will help their neighbors, and those who give with their own hands are following God's commands. If your neighbor is struggling, offer them a loan, and if you borrow, make sure to pay it back on time. Be honest and dependable, and you'll always find help when you need it.

Many people borrow money as if it's a gift and end up causing trouble for those who trusted them. At first, they may act humble and say nice things to win favor. But when it's time to repay, they stall, make excuses, and complain about their bad luck. If they manage to avoid paying back, the lender might be lucky to recover even a small part of what was owed. In worse cases, the borrower takes the money and turns against the lender, showing no gratitude and even responding with insults or accusations.

Because of this, many people stop lending altogether. But don't let this stop you from helping someone in need, and don't make a struggling person wait for help. Give freely when you can and don't send someone away empty-handed. Be willing to take risks to help a friend or a family member. Don't let your money sit idle, going to waste like a stone left unused. Use what you have in ways that honor God's commands, and it will be more valuable than gold. Kindness and generosity are treasures that will protect you in times of trouble. They are stronger than any shield or weapon when it comes to defending you from harm.

A generous person will stand by a neighbor's loan, but someone who lacks integrity will fail to keep their promises. If someone has risked their own money to help you, don't forget their kindness. They may have put everything on the line for your sake. But a careless person will waste the resources of someone who supported them, and an ungrateful person will turn their back on the one who rescued them.

Guaranteeing someone else's loan has ruined many successful people, tossing them around like waves in the sea. Some have lost their homes and been forced to live in foreign lands. A reckless person who makes promises without thinking will end up trapped in legal troubles. Help your neighbor as much as you can, but don't put yourself in danger while doing so.

The basics of life are simple: water, food, clothing, and a home where you can have privacy. It's better to live humbly in a small home of your own than to enjoy luxury while staying as a guest in someone else's house. Whether you have a little or a lot, learn to be content. Moving from place to place is exhausting, especially when you're a guest who doesn't have freedom or comfort.

You might serve food and drinks to your hosts and receive no gratitude in return. Instead, they might speak to you harshly: "Come here, traveler, and serve me." Or worse, they might say, "It's time for you to leave. Someone important is coming. My family is staying over, and I need my space back."

These situations are hard for an understanding person to bear—being scolded for needing a place to stay and suffering the harsh words of those who demand repayment.

Chapter 30

A loving father corrects his child often, making sure he grows up to bring joy. A parent who teaches and disciplines his son will feel proud and gain respect from others. Raising a child well can even make his enemies jealous, and he will feel honored among his friends. Even after the father is gone, it will feel like he still lives on through his son, who reflects his values. While the father is alive, his child brings him happiness, and when he dies, he has no regrets, knowing his son will be strong and kind.

But a parent who spoils their child will always have to deal with the problems that follow, and it will hurt every time the child's bad choices bring trouble. Just like an untrained horse becomes wild, a child without discipline will grow rebellious. If you give a child too much freedom, they will make you worry. If you treat them too casually, they will cause you sadness. Don't joke around too much with them, or you might regret it later. Don't let them do whatever they want when they are young, and don't ignore foolish behavior.

Correct them while they are still young, and guide them with a firm hand. If you don't, they may become disrespectful and bring you shame. Teach them responsibility so they don't grow up without a sense of honor.

A poor man who is strong and healthy is better off than a rich man suffering from illness. Good health and a strong body are more valuable than gold and wealth. There is no treasure greater than being healthy and no joy better than having peace of mind. It is better to die than to live in constant misery, and resting in peace is better than struggling through endless sickness.

Giving gifts to someone who cannot enjoy them is pointless, like offering food to a grave. What is the use of an offering to an idol? It cannot eat or smell. In the same way, those suffering under the Lord's punishment groan in pain, unable to act—like a man longing for a wife but unable to fulfill his desire.

Don't let sadness take over your life, and don't make yourself suffer for no reason. A happy heart gives energy and makes life better, and a cheerful spirit can even help you live longer. Take care of yourself and find peace in your heart. Push sorrow away because it has ruined many lives and does nothing good. Jealousy and anger will shorten your life, and constant stress will make you age faster. Those who are happy and content will enjoy their meals and gain strength from them.

Chapter 31

Constantly worrying about money wears a person down, and stressing over wealth takes away peace of mind. Sleepless nights leave people longing for rest, but even sleep can be disturbed by sickness or anxiety. A rich person works hard to build his fortune, and when he rests, he enjoys the comforts of his wealth. A poor person works just as hard but still struggles, and even when he rests, his hunger remains.

Those who are obsessed with money will always feel guilty, and those who chase after greed will eventually be destroyed by it. Many have ruined their lives by craving riches, bringing disaster upon themselves. Greed is a trap that catches anyone who falls for its temptation. But blessed is the person who stays honest, even when they are wealthy, and does not let greed control their heart.

Who among the rich can truly be called blessed? It is the one who has used his wealth to do good for others. Who has been tested by riches but stayed honest? That person can be proud of his actions. Who had the chance to do wrong but chose to walk away, or could have hurt others but refused? That person will find lasting success and be respected by his community.

If you are invited to a big feast, don't let greed take over. Don't think, "Look at all this food!" Remember, greed is dangerous, and nothing is greedier than the eyes—they are never satisfied and always want more. Don't grab at every dish or reach for whatever looks good. Be considerate of others and show self-control.

Eat a modest amount and don't overindulge, or people might dislike your behavior. Stop eating before you are completely full as a sign of respect. Don't be greedy, or you may embarrass yourself. When eating with others, don't rush to take food before everyone else. A well-mannered person is happy with a small portion and sleeps peacefully. Eating in moderation leads to restful sleep and a clear mind the next morning. But overeating causes discomfort, sleepless nights, and regret.

If you've eaten too much, get up and take a walk—it will help you feel better. Listen to this advice, my child, and don't ignore it. In time, you will see how wise it is. Be thoughtful and disciplined in everything you do, and you'll avoid unnecessary illness. A generous host earns praise, and their kindness is remembered. But a stingy person earns criticism, and their selfishness will not be forgotten.

Don't try to impress others by drinking too much alcohol—it has ruined many lives. Just as fire tests the strength of metal, wine reveals the true character of a proud person in an argument. Wine, when enjoyed in moderation, can bring happiness. What joy is there for someone who never drinks it? It was made to lighten the heart and lift the spirit. But drinking too much leads to bitterness, anger, and fights. Drunkenness turns a fool into his worst self, weakening his body, draining his energy, and leaving him with regret.

At a gathering where wine is served, don't judge your neighbor for drinking or try to embarrass him. Avoid harsh words or demands that might ruin his mood or take away from the joy of the celebration.

Chapter 32

If you are chosen to host a feast, don't let it make you feel more important than others. Treat everyone kindly and make sure your guests are comfortable before you sit down to eat. Once you've taken care of everything, relax and enjoy the company of those around you. Your efforts will be noticed and appreciated.

If you are older, you have the right to speak, but do so wisely. Don't interrupt the music or talk over it. Don't try to show off your knowledge at the wrong time. Music at a feast is like a precious jewel in a golden setting—it adds beauty and value. A pleasant song paired with good wine is like an elegant decoration made of gold and emeralds.

If you are younger and asked to speak, keep your words short and meaningful. Speak only when invited, and don't go on for too long. Act with understanding and know when to stay quiet. If you are with important people, don't try to act like their equal or talk over others.

Just as lightning comes before thunder, respect comes to those who are humble. When the time is right, leave the gathering early instead of overstaying your welcome. Go straight home and enjoy your time there, but don't let pride lead you into wrongdoing. In all things, give thanks to your Creator, who gives you the blessings you enjoy.

Those who respect the Lord will accept correction, and those who seek Him will receive His kindness. Those who follow His law will find peace, but hypocrites will struggle with it. Those who honor the Lord will gain wisdom and shine with goodness.

A sinful person refuses to be corrected and only listens to what benefits them. A wise person values good advice, but a proud person will act foolishly, refusing to admit mistakes or learn from them. Don't act without thinking, and once you make a choice, don't constantly regret it.

Avoid paths that lead to trouble, and don't take risks that aren't necessary. Even when things seem easy, don't become careless—always stay aware. Pay attention to those around you, even your own children. In everything you do, take care of your soul, for this is the key to following the Lord's commands. Those who respect the law will listen to its teachings, and those who trust in the Lord will not be misled.

Chapter 33

No harm will come to those who respect the Lord because even in tough times, He will rescue them again and again. A wise person follows the law, but a hypocrite is as unreliable as a ship caught in a storm. Those who truly understand put their trust in the law, which guides them like a faithful messenger.

Choose your words wisely, and people will listen. Think before you speak, and give thoughtful answers. A fool's mind is restless, like a wheel that spins out of control. His thoughts are as unstable as a cart rolling unevenly. A wild horse is like an undisciplined friend, resisting anyone who tries to guide him.

Why is one day different from another when the same sun shines on all? The Lord, in His wisdom, has set certain days apart. He created seasons and special festivals, making some days sacred while others remain ordinary. All people come from the earth, just like Adam, who was made from dust. The Lord, in His wisdom, made people different and set their paths apart. Some He blessed, raising them to greatness, while others He humbled and brought down.

Just as a potter shapes clay, so the Creator molds people according to His plan. He decides their purpose and judges them as He sees fit. Good and evil oppose each other, just as life and death do. In the same way, sinners stand against the godly. Everything in creation has a balance—each thing has its opposite.

I felt like someone picking up leftover grapes after the harvesters had finished, but the Lord blessed me. My winepress was filled as if I had gathered the grapes myself. Remember, my work was not just for my own benefit but for all who seek wisdom and guidance.

Listen to me, leaders and those who guide others. Do not give control over your life to your son, wife, brother, or friend while you are still alive. Do not hand over your belongings to someone else, or you may regret it later and find yourself asking for them back. As long as you live and have strength, keep control of your life. It is better for your children to depend on you than for you to rely on them. Strive for excellence in all you do, and protect your reputation. When your time comes, distribute your inheritance, but wait until your final days to do so.

Donkeys need food, whips, and burdens, and servants need bread, discipline, and work. Keep your servant busy, and you will have peace. If you leave him idle, he may start thinking about freedom. A yoke and whip keep a servant humble, and strict discipline is needed for those who are disobedient. Keep him occupied, or idleness will lead him to trouble. Give him tasks that suit him, and if he refuses to obey, enforce stricter discipline.

Do not be cruel or unfair to anyone. If you have a servant, treat him with respect because his life was paid for with blood. Value your servant as you value yourself because you depend on him as much as he depends on you. If you mistreat him and he decides to leave, where will you go to find him?

Chapter 34

Empty hopes belong to those who lack understanding, and foolish people are misled by dreams. Chasing dreams is like trying to catch a shadow or follow the wind. Dreams are nothing more than reflections, like one face mirroring another. How can something pure come from what is impure? How can truth come from lies?

Fortune-telling, omens, and dreams are worthless. The mind is filled with illusions, just like the pain of a woman in labor. Unless a dream comes as a message from the Most High, do not trust it. Many have been deceived by dreams, failing because they relied on them too much.

Without lies, the law is fulfilled, and wisdom is found in the words of those who are faithful. A well-taught person understands much, and someone with experience speaks with wisdom. A person with little experience knows little, but those who travel and see the world gain knowledge and perspective. I have witnessed many things on my journeys, and my understanding goes deeper than words can explain. I have faced danger, even the threat of death, but my experiences have guided and protected me.

Those who respect the Lord will thrive because they put their hope in the One who saves them. Whoever fears the Lord will not be weak or afraid, for the Lord is their strength. Blessed is the person who trusts in the Lord. Whose voice does he listen to? Who is his support? The Lord watches over those who love Him. He is their strong protector and steady foundation, their shelter from the heat, their shade at midday, their guide when they stumble, and their help in times of trouble. He lifts their spirits, brightens their eyes, and grants them health, life, and blessings.

Someone who offers a sacrifice from stolen goods disrespects the very act of giving. The sacrifices of wicked people are worthless. The Most High is not pleased with offerings from the ungodly, and no amount of gifts can make up for their sins. It is like killing a child in front of their father while pretending to make an offering. The food of the poor is their life, and taking it from them is like committing murder. Robbing someone of their means to live is like taking their life. Holding back a worker's wages is no different from shedding blood.

If one person builds something and another tears it down, what have they gained but wasted effort? If one prays while another curses, whose prayer will the Lord listen to? A person who washes after touching a dead body but then touches it again has gained nothing from washing. In the same way, someone who fasts for their sins but keeps returning to them gains nothing from fasting. Who will listen to their prayers? What good is their false humility?

Chapter 35

Whoever follows the law is like someone making many offerings, and whoever obeys the commandments gives a gift of peace. Being kind is like offering the finest flour, and helping others is like giving a thank-you offering. Turning away from evil pleases the Lord, and leaving behind sin is like making a sacrifice to make up for past mistakes. Don't come to the Lord empty-handed.

These things should be done because they are His commands. The offerings of good people bring honor to the altar, and their pleasing scent rises up to the Most High. God accepts the sacrifices of those who do what is right, and He will never forget them. Show respect for the Lord by being generous, and don't hold back when giving the first portion of what you earn. When you give, do it with a happy heart, and offer your tithe with joy.

Give to the Most High according to how much He has blessed you. Be as generous as you are able. The Lord rewards kindness, and He will repay you many times over. But don't think you can buy God's favor with gifts—He will not accept them. Don't offer anything gained dishonestly, because the Lord is a fair judge who treats everyone equally.

God does not take sides against the poor, and He listens to the prayers of those who have been wronged. He does not ignore orphans or widows when they cry out for help. Aren't a widow's tears visible on her face? Isn't her sorrow directed at the one who caused her pain?

The person who faithfully serves God will be accepted, and their prayers will reach heaven. The prayers of humble people rise like smoke through the clouds. Their prayers won't stop until they reach the Lord. They keep calling out until the Most High steps in, judges fairly, and brings justice.

The Lord will not wait forever or stay silent without limit. He will break the power of the cruel and bring justice to the nations. He will humble the proud and take away the strength of the wicked. He will repay everyone according to their actions and give them what they deserve based on their choices. He will stand up for His people and bring them joy through His mercy.

Mercy is as valuable in hard times as rain is during a drought.

Chapter 36

Have mercy on us, Lord, the God of all, and show us your kindness. Let the whole world see your power. Show your strength against the nations so they will recognize your might. Just as you revealed your holiness to us, let them now see your greatness through us. Let them understand, as we have come to know, that you alone are God—there is no other.

Show new signs and perform great wonders. Display your power and strengthen your mighty hand. Let your anger rise, and pour out your judgment. Defeat those who oppose you and bring an end to your enemies. Speed up the time you have planned and remember your promises, so that everyone may witness your mighty works. Let those who survive be consumed by fire, and may those who harm your people face their downfall. Crush the rulers of your enemies, those who boast, "We are the only ones who matter."

Bring together all the tribes of Jacob and restore them as your chosen people, just as you did before. Lord, show kindness to those who carry your name, to Israel, your firstborn. Have mercy on the city of your holy temple, Jerusalem, the place where you dwell. Fill

Zion with your majesty, and let your words of truth be honored. Let your people be surrounded by your glory.

Keep the promises you made to those you created from the beginning. Fulfill the prophecies spoken in your name. Reward those who patiently wait for you so that people will trust in your prophets. Lord, listen to the prayers of your servants, just as you gave Aaron the blessing for your people. Let the whole earth know that you are the Lord, the eternal God.

The stomach can handle any food, but some meals taste better than others. The mouth enjoys fresh meat, just as a wise heart can recognize deceitful words. A stubborn heart leads to trouble, but an experienced person knows how to respond wisely.

A woman may accept any man, but some daughters are still better than others. A woman's beauty brightens her face, and nothing is more attractive to a man. If she speaks with kindness and humility, her husband will be admired. A man who finds a good wife has found a priceless treasure—a partner and a source of strength.

Without a fence, a field is open to anyone. In the same way, a man without a wife feels lonely and incomplete. Who would trust a thief who moves from city to city? In the same way, who would rely on a man with no home, who sleeps wherever he can find shelter?

Chapter 37

Everyone will say, "I'm your friend," but some people are only friends in name. Isn't it painful, even unbearable, when someone you trusted turns against you? Deceitful thoughts fill the world with lies—why do they exist?

Some friends celebrate with you when things are good but disappear when trouble comes. Others stay around only for their own gain, but when danger appears, they leave to save themselves. Never forget a true friend, and don't ignore them when life is going well for you.

Every advisor believes their advice is the best, but some only give advice that benefits themselves. Be careful when listening to others, and try to understand their true intentions. They may be looking out for their own interests and waiting to see what happens to you. Don't trust advice from someone who doesn't have faith in you, and don't share your plans with someone who envies you.

Don't ask a woman about her rival, a coward about war, a merchant about business, a buyer about selling, a jealous person about gratitude, a cruel person about kindness, a lazy person about hard work, a servant about completing a job, or an idle worker about serious business. These people won't give trustworthy advice.

Instead, seek advice from someone who follows God's ways, obeys His commandments, and cares about you as much as they care about themselves. Find someone who will stand by you even if you fail. Trust your own judgment as well, because no one knows you better than yourself. Sometimes, your own thoughts can guide you better than a group of watchmen standing guard. But above all, ask God to lead you in truth.

Use reason to make decisions, and think carefully before taking action. Four things test a person's heart: good and evil, life and death. The words we speak hold the power to shape all of them.

Some people teach many but fail to improve themselves. Others are skilled with words but are disliked and end up with nothing. They lack God's favor and miss out on wisdom. But a person who grows wise for their own soul speaks with understanding and earns trust. A wise person teaches others, and their words are dependable. They will receive many blessings, and people will call them fortunate.

A person's life is measured in days, but the days of Israel are countless. A wise person earns the trust of their community, and their name is remembered forever.

My child, reflect on your life and choices. Pay attention to what harms you and avoid it. Not everything is good for everyone, and people have different preferences. Don't overindulge in luxury, and don't be greedy with food. Eating too much can make you sick, and greed brings discomfort. Many have suffered because of their lack of self-control, but those who are mindful live longer.

Chapter 38

Respect doctors when you need their help,
because their skill is a gift from God.
Healing comes from the Lord,
and even kings rely on doctors.
A doctor's knowledge earns them respect,
and they are admired by those in power.

God created medicines from the earth,
and wise people understand their importance.
Didn't He make bitter water sweet with a piece of
    wood,
showing His power through it?
He gave people knowledge
so His wonders could be recognized.
With this knowledge, He heals the sick
and eases the pain of those who suffer.
Pharmacists use this wisdom to prepare medicines,
and through God's work, peace is brought to the
    world.

My child, when you feel sick, don't ignore it.
Pray to God, and He will help you heal.
Turn away from wrongdoing,
and live a good life.
Cleanse your heart of sin.
Offer the best you can as a sacrifice,
and pour oil on it according to your means.
Then, let the doctor do their job,
for they too are part of God's creation.
Don't refuse their help,
because their care might be what you need.
There are times when recovery depends on their
    skills.
Even doctors pray to God,
asking for guidance to heal their patients
and bring life back to them.

But remember, those who offend their Creator
may find themselves in need of a doctor.

My child, cry for those who have passed away.
Mourn them deeply, and show your grief.
Prepare their body with care,
and don't neglect their burial.
Weep from your heart and express your sorrow.
Let your mourning reflect your love for them,
but don't let it last too long—one or two days—

so people don't criticize you.
Then, move forward and find comfort in your
    heart.
Too much grief can weigh you down.
A heavy heart drains your strength.

Grief lingers in difficult times,
and life is even harder for the poor.
Don't let sadness take over your life.
Let go of sorrow,
knowing that death is a natural part of life.
You can't bring someone back once they are gone.
Endless mourning won't help the dead,
but it will only hurt you.
Think about how life ends,
because your time will come too.
Yesterday it was them; tomorrow it could be you.
When the dead find peace, let their memory rest as
    well.
Find comfort as their spirit moves on.

Wisdom comes to those who have time to learn.
People who are free from heavy labor
have more time to gain understanding.
But how can someone grow in wisdom
if they spend their days plowing fields,
finding joy in their oxen,

and only talking about livestock?
They focus on making straight rows,
and their minds are on tending animals.

The same goes for craftsmen and skilled workers.
They labor tirelessly, day and night.
The engraver carefully carves intricate designs,
putting his heart into making beautiful pieces.
The blacksmith hammers hot metal,
shaping iron into useful tools.
The fire burns his skin,
and the sound of pounding fills his ears.
But his eyes stay locked on his creation,
determined to make it perfect.

The potter, working at his wheel,
is completely focused on his craft.
He shapes and molds clay with skilled hands,
creating many useful items.
He carefully applies glaze
and fires his pottery to perfection.

All of these workers depend on their abilities,
and each one is skilled in their trade.
Without them, no city could function.
People wouldn't have homes or roads to walk on.

Translated by Tim Zengerink

But they are not found in places of power.
They don't lead assemblies or interpret laws.
They don't teach wisdom or tell parables.
Even so, their work keeps the world running.
Their prayers are expressed through their skillful
    hands.

Chapter 39

Whoever is dedicated to following the law of the Most High and thinks deeply about it will search for wisdom from the past and study the words of the prophets. They will value the teachings of wise people and seek to understand the hidden meanings in parables. They will learn the deeper lessons behind proverbs and uncover the messages within riddles.

Such a person will stand among great leaders and serve in the presence of rulers. They will travel to different places, learning to distinguish between good and bad in people. Their heart will always turn toward the Lord, their Creator, and they will pray to the Most High, asking for mercy and forgiveness for their mistakes.

If it is God's will, they will be filled with wisdom and understanding. They will speak with insight and offer prayers of gratitude. They will guide others with their knowledge and reflect on the mysteries of God. They will teach the lessons they have learned and take joy in following God's law. Many will respect their wisdom, and their teachings will not be forgotten. Their name will be remembered for generations, and people from different nations will recognize their wisdom. The community of believers will honor them and speak of their knowledge.

If they stay true to their purpose, their reputation will grow beyond even the most successful people. Even after their life ends, their legacy will remain. I have much more to say, for my thoughts are as full as the bright moon. Listen to me, my children, and grow like a rose planted by a flowing stream. Let your fragrance spread like incense, bloom like a lily, and fill the air with a pleasant scent. Sing songs of praise and thank the Lord for His wonderful works.

Lift up His name and raise your voices in gratitude. Praise Him with music and joyful singing, and declare these words of thanks:

"The Lord's works are amazing, and every command is fulfilled at the right time. No one can ask, 'Why is this happening?' or 'Why is that needed?' because in His perfect timing, everything becomes clear. By His word, the waters gathered in one place, and by His command, the reservoirs were formed. His power makes all things happen, and nothing can stop His salvation.

"Everything people do is visible to Him; nothing is hidden from His sight. From eternity to eternity, He sees all things, and His wisdom covers everything. No one can question, 'Why is this so?' or 'Why is that needed?' because everything serves a purpose. His blessings flow like rivers, pouring over the earth like a flood. Just as He made the sea salty, He has reserved His judgment for those who do evil.

"His ways are clear to those who are faithful, but they are stumbling blocks for those who reject Him. From the beginning, good things were made for those who do right, while destruction was set aside for those who choose sin. The necessities of life—water, fire, iron, salt, flour, honey, milk, wine, oil, and clothing—were created for everyone's benefit. For the godly, these are blessings, but for those who turn away from God, these things can bring harm.

"The winds were made to carry out His justice, and in their fury, they bring punishment. On the day of judgment, they will act with full force to carry out the will of their Creator. Fire, hail, famine, and death—all were created as instruments of His justice. Wild animals, scorpions, snakes, and the sword exist to punish the wicked. They stand ready to obey His commands and will act when the time comes. They never fail to carry out His will."

This is what I have learned from the beginning, and I have carefully written it down after much thought: Everything the Lord does is good, and He provides what is needed at the right time. No one can say, "This is better than that," because everything is perfect when used as He intended.

So now, with all your heart and voice, sing praises and bless the name of the Lord!

Chapter 40

Life is a heavy burden that everyone must carry, passed down from the first human to every person born after. From the moment a baby is born until they return to the earth, life is full of struggles. People worry about what will happen next and fear the certainty of death.

It doesn't matter if someone is a king sitting on a throne or a poor person covered in dirt, if they wear royal robes or simple rags—everyone feels anger, jealousy, anxiety, and the fear of death. Their troubles never leave them, filling their days with stress and their nights with restless thoughts. Even in bed, sleep does not bring peace. Their dreams are filled with fears, like someone standing guard in the dark, afraid of what might come. Their heart pounds as if they are running from battle, only to wake up and realize their fears were for nothing.

Death, violence, arguments, war, disasters, hunger, suffering, and disease affect every living creature—both humans and animals—but sinners feel their weight even more. These evils exist because of the wicked, and they were the reason for the great flood. Everything that comes from the earth will return to it, just as everything that comes from water will return to the sea.

Corruption and injustice will not last forever, but faithfulness will never disappear. The riches of the wicked will dry up like a river during a drought, and their success will vanish like the sound of thunder after a storm. Generous people find joy in giving, but those who live without morals will eventually fall. The children of the wicked will not flourish, like weak roots struggling to grow on dry ground. Just as reeds by the water are pulled up before other plants, the ungodly will not stand strong for long.

Acts of kindness are like a garden full of blessings, and generosity creates a legacy that will never fade. A hardworking and content person enjoys their life, but discovering a hidden treasure is even better. Children and building a city bring honor, but a good and faithful spouse is more valuable than either. Music and wine bring joy to the heart, but the love of wisdom is even greater. A flute and a harp make beautiful sounds, but a kind and gentle voice is even sweeter.

The eye is drawn to beauty and grace, but nothing is more valuable than a field full of ripe crops. A friend or companion brings happiness, but the love between a husband and wife is even stronger. Relatives and helpers are useful in times of trouble, but giving to those in need is the best protection of all. Gold and silver can bring stability, but good advice is worth even more. Wealth and strength may lift a person's confidence, but having deep respect for the Lord is more important than both. The fear of the Lord fulfills every need, and those who have it will never go without. It is like a garden full of blessings and gives more honor than anything else.

My child, do not live by begging from others. It is better to die than to rely on people for everything. A person who depends on others for food can never truly live freely. Taking what belongs to someone else brings shame, but a wise and disciplined person avoids this disgrace. For those who lack self-respect, begging may feel easy at first, but it leads to deep humiliation and never-ending hunger.

Chapter 41

Oh, death, how hard it is to think about you for someone who is happy, with no troubles to worry about, enjoying success, good health, and all the pleasures of life. But for the poor and weak, for the elderly who are exhausted and have endured many hardships, death comes as a relief.

Don't be afraid when death calls. Think of all the people who lived before you and those who will come after. This is the path the Lord has set for every living thing. Why fight it when it is part of His plan? Whether someone lives ten years, a hundred, or even a thousand, no one can question the judgment that comes after life.

The children of wicked people often live in disgrace and among those who do evil. Their legacy fades away, and their descendants bear the shame of their actions forever. Children will blame a sinful parent because they suffer the consequences of their wrongdoing. How terrible it is for those who reject the law of the Most High! If they are born, they live under a curse, and when they die, the curse follows them. Everything that comes from the earth returns to the earth, and the wicked will pass from one misery to another.

People mourn over the bodies of the dead, but the wicked will be forgotten. Guard your reputation, for it is more valuable than gold or silver. A good life has an end, but a good name lasts forever.

My children, seek wisdom with an open and calm heart. But what good is wisdom if it is hidden, or wealth if it is never used? A fool who stays silent about his ignorance is better than a wise person who refuses to share knowledge. Pay attention to my words, for not every kind of shame is worth keeping, and not every action is honorable.

Be ashamed of doing wrong in front of your parents, of lying to a leader or someone in authority, of committing crimes before a judge or in public, of betraying a friend or partner, and of stealing while being a guest in someone's home. Be ashamed of dishonoring God's truth and breaking His covenant, of bad manners at the dinner table, or of being rude when giving or receiving gifts. Be ashamed of ignoring someone's greeting, staring at a prostitute, neglecting a relative in need, or taking back something you already gave. Do not look at another man's wife or interfere with his servant—stay far away from his home.

Do not be rude to your friends, and after giving a gift, do not humiliate the person who received it. Avoid gossip and revealing secrets. Only feel shame for things that are truly disgraceful, and you will earn the respect and admiration of others.

Chapter 42

Do not be ashamed of these things, and never commit a sin just to protect your reputation: respecting the law of the Most High and keeping His covenant, ensuring justice even when judging the guilty, settling financial matters fairly with a business partner or fellow traveler, accepting what is rightfully yours from a friend's inheritance, using honest scales and weights in all transactions, being fair in your dealings with merchants, correcting your children regularly, and disciplining a disobedient servant when necessary.

If your wife is untrustworthy, keeping important things secured is wise. When many hands are involved, make sure to safeguard your belongings. Always count and measure carefully when giving or receiving something, and keep a written record of all exchanges.

Don't be afraid to teach those who lack knowledge, even if they are older or disagree with younger people. Helping others learn will increase your own wisdom and earn you respect. A daughter can cause endless worry for her father, making him anxious at every stage of her life. When she is young, he fears she may never marry. If she does, he worries that her husband will mistreat her. While she is still at home, he fears she might make mistakes or become pregnant. If she marries, he hopes she will be faithful and have children, but he constantly worries about her future.

Keep a close watch on a rebellious daughter, or she could bring shame to your name and damage your reputation. She might become the subject of gossip, making people talk badly about you in public. Do not let yourself be distracted by every attractive person, and don't spend too much time in the company of women. Just as moths destroy clothing, a woman's bad influence can spread quickly to others.

It is better to deal with a man's wickedness than to experience the so-called kindness of a woman who brings shame and dishonor. Now I will speak about the works of the Lord and share what I have learned. His creations are revealed through His word. The sun shines brightly, watching over everything, and all His works are filled with His glory.

No one can fully understand all of God's amazing works. He has carefully designed everything, filling the world with beauty and order. He knows the deepest parts of the earth and the hidden thoughts in every heart. Nothing is a mystery to Him because the Most High sees and understands all things. He knows the signs of the world, reveals the past, predicts the future, and uncovers what is hidden.

No thought is hidden from Him, and no word escapes His notice. With His wisdom, He controls everything. He is eternal, with no beginning or end. Nothing can be added to His creation, and nothing has been taken away. He needs no help or guidance.

His works are beyond imagination! Even the smallest detail of creation reflects His greatness. Everything He has made will last forever and serves its purpose according to His plan. All things follow His commands. Everything exists in pairs, balancing and complementing each other. Nothing He made is incomplete—one thing helps explain and complete another. Who can fully understand the greatness of His glory?

Chapter 43

The bright sky is like a crown in the heavens, showing the beauty of creation in all its glory. When the sun rises, it announces the start of a new day. It is a stunning masterpiece made by the Most High. By midday, its heat dries the earth. Who can stand its blazing intensity? A person near a furnace feels extreme heat, but the sun's power is even greater, heating up mountains, sending out fiery rays, and shining so brightly that it dazzles and blinds the eyes.

How amazing is the Lord who created the sun! By His command, it moves quickly across the sky, completing its journey. The moon helps mark time, setting seasons and acting as a sign for the world. It signals special days and celebrations as its light grows and fades. The months are named after the moon, which follows its cycle of waxing and waning. It is one of the great lights in the heavens, shining beautifully in the sky.

The moon and stars sparkle like jewels, lighting up the heights of creation. At the Lord's command, they stay in perfect order, never failing in their purpose. Look at the rainbow and give praise to the One who made it. Its colors are breathtaking, stretching across the sky in a perfect arc, placed there by the hands of the Most High.

By His word, snow falls, and flashes of lightning carry out His will. He opens the skies, and clouds scatter like birds in flight. By His power, heavy clouds form, and hail falls when He commands. When He shows His presence, mountains tremble. At His word, warm winds blow. His thunder shakes the earth, and northern storms bring powerful winds. Snow falls gently like birds descending and covers the ground like swarms of locusts.

The brightness of snow catches the eye, filling hearts with wonder. Frost spreads across the land like salt, and icy landscapes sparkle like crystal. Cold winds freeze the waters, turning ponds and streams into solid ice. The cold burns the mountains, dries the wilderness, and scorches the grass like fire. But then mist rises to heal the earth, and after the heat, dew refreshes and cools the land.

With His wisdom, He calms the deep seas and places islands in their positions. Sailors who travel the oceans speak of its dangers, and we are amazed by the stories they tell. The sea is full of wonders—creatures of all kinds, from the smallest to the largest, even massive sea monsters. At His command, His messengers complete their tasks, and by His word, everything stays in order.

Even if we spoke forever about His works, we could never fully describe them. All we can say is, "He is everything!" Who has the power to give Him the praise He truly deserves? He is greater than all He has created. The Lord is incredible beyond understanding. His power is more than we can imagine.

Praise the Lord and lift Him up as much as you can! Even then, He is greater than your praise. Give Him glory with all your strength and never stop, because no amount of praise will ever be enough. Who has seen Him completely to describe Him? Who can honor Him as He truly deserves? There is so much about Him we cannot see; we have only glimpsed a small part of His works. The Lord is the creator of all things, and He gives wisdom to those who honor Him.

Chapter 44

Let's take a moment to remember and honor the great people of the past—our ancestors from every generation. The Lord blessed them and showed His power through them since the beginning of time. Some were strong and wise rulers who led their nations with wisdom, gave good advice, and had great understanding. Others were prophets who spoke God's truth.

Some guided their people with wisdom, teaching them valuable lessons and sharing their knowledge. Their words were full of insight and instruction. Some used their creativity to make music and write poetry, expressing their thoughts beautifully. Others were gifted with wealth and skill, living peaceful and successful lives.

All of these people were respected while they lived and were admired in their time. Some left behind names that are still remembered today, and their praises continue to be spoken. But others have faded from history, as if they had never lived. They passed away without a lasting record, and so did their children after them.

Still, these were kind and compassionate people, and their good deeds will never be forgotten. Their legacy continues through their descendants, who remain part of God's covenant. Their families stand strong, and because of them, their lineage carries on. Their descendants will last for generations, and their honor will never fade.

Even though their bodies rest in peace, their names are remembered by those who come after them. People continue to celebrate their wisdom, and their praises are shared among the community.

Enoch pleased God and was taken up to heaven, serving as a lasting example of repentance. Noah was a good and righteous man. During a time of judgment, he saved humanity by building the ark, preserving life during the great flood. Because of him, God made an everlasting promise that the earth would never again be destroyed by a flood.

Abraham was a great leader, the father of many nations, unmatched in honor. He followed God's law and entered into a special covenant with Him. He kept his faith even when tested, proving his loyalty.

Because of this, God confirmed His promise to Abraham with an oath, saying that all nations would be blessed through his descendants. He promised to make Abraham's family as countless as the dust of the earth and the stars in the sky, giving them land stretching from sea to sea, from the Euphrates River to the farthest parts of the earth.

This promise was passed down to Isaac because of Abraham's faith, ensuring that the blessing and covenant would continue. That same blessing was given to Jacob, whom God chose and greatly favored. God gave Jacob an inheritance and divided it among the twelve tribes of Israel.

Chapter 45

God chose a man full of kindness and favor, someone loved by both Him and the people. That man was Moses, whose memory is forever honored. The Lord gave Moses great authority, placing him among His most faithful servants, and even lifted him up in front of his enemies. Through Moses, God performed amazing miracles and made him a leader who stood before kings. The Lord trusted him with His commandments and allowed him to experience a part of His divine presence.

Because of Moses' deep faith and humility, God set him apart from everyone else. The Lord spoke directly to him, allowed him to witness His power in the thick clouds, and gave him His laws face to face. These laws—the foundation of knowledge and life—were given to Moses to teach Jacob's descendants and to guide Israel in following God's ways.

God also chose Aaron, Moses' brother from the tribe of Levi, to serve as a holy priest. He made an everlasting covenant with Aaron, granting him the role of high priest for His people. Aaron was given great honor and dressed in sacred robes. His garments were beautifully made—fine linen, a long robe, and the ephod, all designed with skill. The hem of his robe had golden bells and pomegranates, so their sound could be heard in the temple, reminding Israel of God's presence.

Aaron wore special garments decorated with gold, blue, and purple, embroidered with great skill. He carried the Urim and Thummim, used for making judgments. His robe was woven with scarlet threads, and he wore gemstones engraved with the names of Israel's tribes, set in gold. On his turban was a golden crown with the words "HOLINESS," a symbol of honor, carefully crafted by skilled hands. Before Aaron, no one had ever worn such robes, and they were reserved for him and his descendants forever.

Aaron was responsible for offering daily sacrifices to God, twice a day without fail. Moses anointed Aaron with holy oil, dedicating him and his family to serve as priests for all time. Aaron was chosen to stand before the Lord, bless the people, and present offerings to God. Out of all the people, he alone was given the duty of offering sacrifices, burning incense, and making atonement for the nation.

The Lord gave Aaron the responsibility of teaching His laws and sharing His commands with Israel. However, in the wilderness, certain outsiders—Dathan, Abiram, and Korah's followers—grew jealous and rebelled against Aaron. Their actions angered the Lord, who responded with a powerful judgment, destroying them with fire and proving His authority.

Even after this, God continued to bless Aaron by granting him a special portion of Israel's offerings. He received the best of the people's harvests and was provided with food from the sacrifices. Aaron and his descendants were given their share from the offerings, just as God had commanded. However, Aaron did not receive a land inheritance like the other tribes, because the Lord Himself was his reward.

Phinehas, Aaron's grandson and the son of Eleazar, was greatly honored for standing up for God's covenant when the people turned away from Him. Because of Phinehas' actions, he helped restore Israel's faith, and God made a lasting promise of peace with him. Phinehas was given leadership over the sanctuary and the people, and his descendants were promised the priesthood forever.

The Lord also made a covenant with David, the son of Jesse, from the tribe of Judah. The kingship was passed down through his descendants for generations. In the same way, Aaron's priesthood was preserved for his family line. May the Lord give you wisdom to lead His people with fairness, so they remain blessed and their honor lasts for generations to come.

Chapter 46

Joshua, the son of Nun, was a strong and courageous leader who followed Moses as a prophet. Just as his name means "salvation," he led God's people to victory, defeating their enemies and securing the land promised to Israel. How powerful he was when he lifted his hands and fought with his sword against cities! No one could stand as firm as Joshua because the Lord gave him victory over his enemies.

At his command, didn't the sun stop in the sky? Didn't one day seem to last twice as long? Surrounded by his enemies, Joshua called out to the Most High, and God answered him. The Lord sent massive hailstones to strike down the enemy, destroying those who fought against Him. Through these miracles, the nations saw the power of the Lord and realized that Joshua fought under God's guidance because he was faithful to Him.

Even during Moses' time, Joshua proved his loyalty. He and Caleb, the son of Jephunneh, stood against those who rebelled. They encouraged the people to trust in God and silenced their complaints. Out of the 600,000 Israelites who left Egypt, only Joshua and Caleb lived to enter the promised land, the land flowing with milk and honey. The Lord gave Caleb strength even in his old age, allowing him to conquer the hill country that became the inheritance of his descendants. This showed all of Israel that those who follow the Lord will be blessed.

The judges of Israel, whose names are remembered with honor, were those who remained faithful to God and kept their hearts pure. May their memory be cherished! May they rise again, and may their legacy continue through their children.

Samuel, the prophet of the Lord, was deeply loved by God and played a key role in choosing leaders for Israel. He ruled the nation according to God's law, and through him, the Lord watched over His people. Because of his faithfulness, Samuel proved to be a true prophet, and everything he spoke was confirmed by his visions.

When enemies surrounded Israel, Samuel cried out to the Lord and offered a lamb as a sacrifice. God answered him with a loud thunder from heaven, shaking the earth with His mighty voice. He struck down the rulers of the Tyrians and defeated the Philistine leaders.

Before he died, Samuel stood before the people and their king, declaring, "I have taken nothing from anyone—not even a sandal." No one could accuse him of wrongdoing. Even after his death, his prophetic words remained powerful. He predicted the downfall of the king and spoke from the grave, warning the people about their sins and calling them back to God.

Chapter 47

After him, Nathan became a prophet during David's reign. Just like the best part of an offering is set aside, David was chosen and set apart from the people of Israel. He fought lions as if they were goats and wrestled bears as if they were lambs.

As a young man, didn't David defeat a giant and remove the shame from his people? With just a sling, he struck down the proud Goliath. He called on the Most High, and God gave him the strength to defeat a mighty warrior and restore his nation's honor. The people celebrated his victories, praising him for the blessings of the Lord when a glorious crown was placed on his head.

David crushed his enemies from every side, defeating the Philistines and breaking their power so completely that it remains broken to this day. In everything he did, he gave thanks to the Holy One. He glorified God with his songs and poured his whole heart into praising his Creator.

He appointed singers to stand before the altar, filling the temple with beautiful music. He made the festivals more joyful and carefully planned times of worship to honor God's holy name. Their songs filled the sanctuary from early morning. The Lord forgave David's sins and strengthened him for all time. God made an everlasting covenant with him, ensuring that his descendants would rule from a glorious throne in Israel.

After David, his wise son took the throne, and because of David's faithfulness, this son ruled peacefully. Solomon's reign was marked by peace because the Lord gave him rest from his enemies. This gave Solomon the opportunity to build a temple for God's name and establish a sanctuary meant to last forever.

Solomon, how amazing was your wisdom when you were young! You were like an overflowing river of understanding. Your influence spread everywhere, filling the world with proverbs and wise sayings. Your reputation reached distant lands, and people admired you for the peace you brought to your kingdom. Nations were drawn to your songs, your proverbs, and your ability to explain mysteries.

By the power of the Lord, you gathered gold as if it were tin and silver as if it were as common as lead. But you let yourself be controlled by women, and they led you astray. Because of this, your honor was ruined, and your descendants became corrupted. Your actions brought God's anger upon your children. It is painful to see that your mistakes led to the division of the kingdom and the rise of rebellion in Ephraim.

Even so, the Lord did not take away His mercy. He did not destroy His people or erase the descendants of His chosen ones. He remained faithful to those who loved Him, keeping a remnant of Jacob's descendants and preserving a branch from David's family.

When Solomon died, his son Rehoboam took the throne, but he was foolish. His lack of wisdom embarrassed his people. His poor decisions caused the kingdom to rebel against him. Then came Jeroboam, the son of Nebat, who led Israel into sin, causing Ephraim to follow a corrupt path. Their sins kept increasing until they were finally removed from the land. They embraced all kinds of wickedness, and in the end, judgment came upon them.

Chapter 48

Elijah was a prophet whose presence burned like fire, and his words shone as brightly as a torch. Because of his deep passion for God, he brought famine to the land and reduced the number of its people. By the Lord's command, he stopped the rain, and three times, fire came down from heaven at his word.

Elijah, your deeds were truly amazing! Who could compare to you? You brought the dead back to life, saving them from the grave by the power of the Most High. You overthrew kings and healed the sick. You heard God's voice at Mount Sinai and received His commands at Horeb. You anointed kings to carry out justice and appointed prophets to continue your mission.

You were taken up to heaven in a whirlwind, riding a chariot pulled by fiery horses. Your name was meant to bring correction at the right time, to calm God's anger before it fully erupted, to bring peace between fathers and sons, and to restore the tribes of Israel. Blessed are those who saw your greatness and experienced your kindness—they were truly fortunate.

Elijah was carried away in a whirlwind, and his spirit was passed down to Elisha. Elisha was fearless, and no ruler could stand against him. Nothing was too difficult for him. Even after his death, his power continued, and miracles still happened because of him. His life was full of wonders, and even after he was gone, his deeds amazed people.

But despite these incredible signs, the people did not change. They refused to turn from their sins until they were defeated and taken captive, scattered across different lands. Only a small group remained, led by a ruler from David's family. Some of them did what was right, but many continued to do wrong.

Hezekiah strengthened his city and built a water system. He cut through solid rock with iron tools and made reservoirs to store water. During his reign, Sennacherib invaded and sent his commander, Rabshakeh, who spoke arrogantly and threatened Zion. The people were terrified, as if they were in the pains of childbirth.

But they cried out to the merciful Lord, lifting their hands in prayer. The Holy One heard them from heaven and rescued them through the prophet Isaiah. God struck down the Assyrian army, and His angel wiped them out completely. Hezekiah pleased the Lord by following the ways of his ancestor David, listening to the guidance of Isaiah the prophet, who was wise and faithful in his visions.

During Hezekiah's time, the sun moved backward, and his life was extended. Isaiah, filled with a remarkable spirit, saw visions of the future and brought comfort to those grieving in Zion. He revealed events that would happen, even to the end of time, showing hidden things before they took place.

Chapter 49

The memory of Josiah is like a sweet-smelling incense, carefully crafted by a skilled maker. His goodness was as delightful as honey on the tongue and as joyful as music at a celebration. Josiah did what was right, leading the people back to God and removing sinful practices from the land. He devoted himself fully to serving the Lord and stayed faithful, even when the world around him was filled with corruption.

Unlike David, Hezekiah, and Josiah, most of the other kings of Judah turned away from God's laws. Because of their wickedness, they lost their thrones, and foreign nations took over their kingdom. Strangers ruled over them, and their honor was stripped away. They burned down the holy city and left its streets empty, just as the prophet Jeremiah had warned.

Jeremiah was chosen by God before he was even born. Though he faced much suffering, he was called to deliver God's message—to tear down and destroy what was wrong but also to rebuild and restore what was good. Ezekiel, another great prophet, was given a vision of God's glory. He saw the Lord's presence through the chariot of the cherubim. He spoke of God's judgment on enemies and brought blessings to those who followed the right path.

May the bones of the twelve prophets rest in peace, for they gave hope and courage to the people of Israel. How can we ever give enough praise to Zerubbabel? He was like a seal on God's right hand, chosen for a special purpose. The same can be said of Jesus, the son of Josedek, who helped rebuild the Lord's temple and guided the people back to holiness, preparing them for eternal glory.

Nehemiah also deserves great honor. He restored the broken walls of the city, rebuilt its gates, and gave the people back their homes. No one on earth has ever been like Enoch, who was taken up from the earth. No one has been like Joseph, who became a leader and protector of his people. Even after his death, his bones were treated with the highest respect.

Shem and Seth were greatly honored among men, but above all creation, Adam was set apart.

Chapter 50

Simon, son of Onias, was a high priest who dedicated his life to restoring God's temple and making it stronger. During his time, he built up the foundations, reinforced the double walls, and raised the great enclosures of the temple. He also oversaw the construction of a huge water reservoir and a massive bronze basin as wide as the sea. He worked hard to protect his people from disaster and fortified the city so it could withstand enemy attacks.

How magnificent he was when he appeared before the people, stepping out from behind the temple's veil! He shined like the morning star breaking through the clouds, like the full moon glowing at its brightest, and like the sun beaming over the Lord's temple. He was as stunning as a rainbow in the clouds, as beautiful as roses blooming in early spring, as fresh as lilies by a flowing stream, and as fragrant as a tree full of frankincense in summer. He was like the bright fire of burning incense, like a golden bowl covered in shining jewels, like an olive tree heavy with fruit, and like a tall cypress tree reaching into the sky.

When Simon wore his sacred robes, dressed in all his splendor, and stepped up to the holy altar, the sanctuary seemed to glow with glory. As he received offerings from the priests, standing with his fellow ministers like a wreath surrounding him, he was as majestic as a cedar tree in Lebanon, standing tall among towering palm trees. The priests, the sons of Aaron, stood in their sacred garments, holding the Lord's offerings before the entire assembly of Israel.

When the service at the altar was finished, Simon carefully arranged the offering for the Almighty. He lifted his hands to the cup of wine and poured it at the base of the altar as a sweet offering to the King of all. Then the sons of Aaron sounded the trumpets of hammered silver, their music filling the air to honor the Most High.

The people bowed low in worship, pressing their faces to the ground before the Almighty God. The singers raised their voices in praise, and the entire temple was filled with the sound of beautiful music. The people cried out to the Lord, calling upon His mercy, and they remained in prayer until the sacred ceremony was complete.

Afterward, Simon stepped down and raised his hands over the entire congregation of Israel, blessing them in the name of the Lord and lifting up His holy name. He bowed again in worship and declared a blessing from the Most High:

"Let us bless the God of all, who performs wonders everywhere, who formed us in the womb and continues to show us His kindness. May He fill our hearts with joy and grant us peace in Israel for all generations. May His mercy be with us, and may He save us at the perfect time."

My soul is troubled by two nations, and there is a third that I don't even consider a nation: those who live on the mountains of Samaria, the Philistines, and the foolish people of Shechem.

I, Jesus, the son of Sirach, Eleazar of Jerusalem, have written this book filled with wisdom and understanding, sharing knowledge from my heart. Blessed is the one who follows these teachings. Whoever treasures them will grow wise, and by putting them into practice, they will gain strength in all things. The light of the Lord will guide their path.

Chapter 51

A Prayer of Jesus, the son of Sirach.

I thank you, Lord, my King, and I praise you, my God and Savior. I am grateful for your name because you have always protected and helped me. You have saved me from danger and rescued me from the lies and traps of those who spread false stories. You stood by my side, saving me with your endless mercy and the power of your name.

You delivered me from those who were ready to attack me, from people who wanted to harm me. You saved me from many troubles, from the fire that surrounded me, and from flames I did not cause. You pulled me back from the edge of death, from false accusations and the words of those who slandered me in front of the king.

My soul was close to death, and my life was nearly over. I was trapped on all sides, and no one could help me. I looked for someone to save me, but there was no one. Then I remembered your mercy, Lord, and your promises that last forever. You save those who wait for you and protect them from their enemies.

I lifted my prayer from the earth, begging to be rescued from death. I called on the Lord, the Father of my Lord, asking Him not to leave me alone in my time of trouble, when no one else would stand up for me. I will praise your name forever and sing songs of thanks because you heard my prayer.

You saved me from destruction and delivered me in my darkest moments. Because of this, I will praise you, bless your name, and glorify the Lord.

When I was young, before I had much experience, I searched for wisdom through prayer. I asked for her guidance near the temple, and I will continue to seek her until my last day.

From my early days until now, my heart has been filled with joy because of wisdom. I have walked with honesty and followed her path since my youth. By listening carefully, I gained great wisdom for myself. She has been a great benefit to me, and I will give glory to the one who gives wisdom.

I was determined to follow her, eager to do what is good, and I have no regrets. My soul struggled to gain her, and I worked hard in my efforts. I lifted my hands to heaven and grieved over my lack of understanding. I focused my heart on wisdom, and in purity, I found her. From the beginning, I dedicated myself to her, and because of this, I will never be abandoned.

I faced many struggles in my search for wisdom, but in return, I found something priceless. The Lord rewarded me with the gift of speech, and I will use it to praise Him.

Come close to me, all who lack understanding, and make your home in the house of wisdom. Why do you still lack what you need? Your souls thirst deeply for wisdom. I opened my mouth and said, "Gain wisdom without spending money. Take her teachings upon yourself, and let your soul embrace her instruction. She is easy to find.

See for yourselves that I put in only a little effort, but I gained much peace. Seek wisdom as if you were buying silver, and through her, you will receive wealth greater than gold. Let your soul rejoice in the Lord's mercy, and never be ashamed to praise Him.

Complete your work before your time runs out, and at the right moment, He will reward you."

Thank You for Reading

Dear Reader,

We hope this timeless classic has sparked your imagination and enriched your literary journey. Now that you've turned the final page, we want to share a vision for the future of reading—one where every classic you've ever wanted to explore is at your fingertips, in a format that best suits your life.

We'd like to invite you to gain immediate, unlimited digital & audiobook access to hundreds of the most treasured literary classics ever written—along with the option to secure deluxe paperback, hardcover & box set editions at printing cost. Together, we can spark a new global literary renaissance alongside our small, independent publishing house called "The Library of Alexandria."

Thousands of years ago, the Library of Alexandria stood as a beacon of knowledge—until it was lost to history. We aim to reignite that spirit of preservation and discovery right now, in the modern age—only this time, it's accessible to all, in every language and every format.

Picture a world where every timeless classic, novel, poem, or philosophical treatise is not only available to read but also updated for today's readers—modernized, translated into any language or dialect, and ready to enjoy in any format you choose, whether that is in an eBook, audiobook, paperback, or deluxe hardcover & box set version a printing cost.

By joining our movement to rebuild the modern Library of Alexandria, you become part of an unprecedented mission to offer:

- **Unlimited Audiobook & eBook Access to the Greatest Classics of All Time**

  Instantly explore thousands of legendary works, from Plato and Shakespeare to Jane Austen and Leo Tolstoy. All are instantly ready to read or listen to, giving you a complete literary universe at your fingertips.

- **Paperback & Deluxe Editions at Printing Costs:**

  Purchase any title in a paperback, deluxe hardbound, or deluxe boxset edition at printing costs, shipped right to your doorstep. Curate your personal library of Alexandria with editions worthy of display—crafted to last, designed to captivate, and delivered straight to your door.

- **Modern translations for Contemporary Readers in all languages and dialects**

  Discover a vast selection of classics reimagined in clear, current language—no more struggling with outdated phrases or obscure references. Next to the original versions, we aim to offer translations in as many languages and dialects as possible.

  As we continue our translation efforts and add new languages, readers everywhere can connect with these works as if they were written today. By bridging linguistic divides, you're contributing to ensuring that these timeless stories become more meaningful, accessible, and inspiring for people across the globe.

- **Your Personal Library of Alexandria:**

  Over the months and years, you'll curate a unique physical archive of classics—each volume a testament to your taste, curiosity, and love of knowledge. It's not just about owning books—it's about curating a cultural legacy you'll cherish and pass down for generations to come.

- **Join a Global Literary Renaissance:**

  Your support fuels an ongoing mission: allowing us to reinvest in offering deluxe print editions (including special boxsets) at their true cost, broaden the range of available formats and translations, and extend the reach of these works to new audiences worldwide. By joining today, you're not just preserving a legacy of masterpieces; you set in motion a powerful wave of literary accessibility.

We are more than a publisher—we're a movement, and we can't do it alone. Your support lets us scale our mission, preserving and reimagining history's greatest works for tomorrow's readers.

Become a Torchbearer of knowledge.

Thank you for picking up this book and allowing us into your literary journey. As you turn the pages, know that you're part of something larger: a global effort to keep these stories alive, share their wisdom across borders and generations, and spark a true cultural revival for the modern era.

If this resonates with you—please consider taking the next step by visiting:

www.libraryofalexandria.com

With gratitude and a shared love of knowledge,

The Modern Library of Alexandria Team

Visit:

www.libraryofalexandria.com

Or scan the code below: